The Legends of Louisiana
Cookbook

By
Sheila E. Ainbinder

A FIRESIDE BOOK
PUBLISHED BY SIMON & SCHUSTER INC.
NEW YORK, LONDON, TORONTO,
SYDNEY, TOKYO, SINGAPORE

Dedication
In memory of George deVille

To Harvey, my best friend and toughest critic; Hollie, my P.R. person and collaborator; Marci, my computer expert; Stacey, my business consultant; and Terri, my righthand woman, without whose dedication this book could not have happened.

Acknowledgments
Editing—Sheila Ainbinder and Marian Levine
Illustrations—Jennifer Barrett

Fireside
Simon & Schuster Building
Rockefeller Center
1230 Avenue of the Americas
New York, New York 10020

First Fireside Edition, 1991
Published by arrangement with the author

FIRESIDE and colophon are registered trademarks
of Simon & Schuster Inc.

Manufactured in the United States of America

10 9 8 7 6 5 4 3 2 1 Pbk.

Library of Congress Cataloging in Publication Data
Ainbinder, Sheila E.
  The legends of Louisiana cookbook/by Sheila E. Ainbinder.—1st
Fireside ed.
    p.   cm.
  "A Fireside book."
  Reprint. Originally published: Silver Spring, MD: American Cooking Guild, © 1987.
  Includes index.
  1. Cookery, American—Louisiana style.   I. Title.
TX715.2.L68A48   1991
641.59763—dc20   90-40840
                                                            CIP
ISBN 0-671-70817-1   Pbk.

Table Of Contents

*Appropriate Recipes Follow Each Legend
For Alphabetical Listing of Recipes See Index*

Introduction

I found myself, a Yankee from Maryland (with New York roots), living in New Orleans, Louisiana for two years, while working on Riverwalk Marketplace. During this time, I grew to love the city and it's people.

New Orleans is a city of a million people, with a best selling book called the "200 Best Restaurants of New Orleans." (What a dead giveaway about the quantity and quality of good food there!) It's a place that feels more like a European town than a southern city. In fact, a friend who has lived there since 1982 told me that he "left the U.S. and moved to New Orleans five years ago." Just when you start to understand that statement, you meet someone from the ninth ward who sounds like they're from my old neighborhood in Brooklyn.

In New Orleans, if two people meet on a street corner, there's a good chance they'll have a party. If three people meet, it's cause for a parade!

These folks love to laugh at themselves, but they take two things very seriously; their politics and their food. Table talk at dinner not only includes what was eaten at one's last meal, the hopes and expectations for this meal, but first and foremost, where and what will one eat tomorrow. Maybe that's why the place has the distinction of being the only metropolitan area I know of with recipes in the telephone directory, and the only city with its own cuisine. (Did you ever hear of Dallas cuisine, or Cincinnati cuisine. . . . even New York cuisine?)

Having eaten my way through the city and practically through the state (with the only saving grace being my aerobics class), I look at this book as part of a natural progression. It is from the people of the city; about themselves, their history and most importantly, their food. It is, in fact, a book of wonderful stories that happens to have some of the best recipes in the world. They have been tried by the chefs themselves and if followed correctly, should prove successful. I hope it is as much fun to read and use as it has been to put together.

Special Thanks

Special thanks to Rick Evans, Cathy Case, Joe Piccolomini, Carol Lentz and Gina Lewis from The Rouse Company's Riverwalk for their assistance and support throughout the process of putting together the *Legends of Louisiana Cookbook.*

There are so many people who are part of this book—those who contributed their time, thoughts, recipes and anecdotes—I am grateful to them all. Individually I want to thank Bill Cates and The American Cooking Guild for all their help; Arlene Gillis and Marsha Berman for their good advice; Ella Brennan, for her recipes and stories and for just being a friend; Mel Leavitt, for sharing his infinite knowledge of this wonderful city; Joan and Rick Pyle, for their help and their daughter; the entire Roy family for feeding me whenever I come "home" to New Orleans; and Larry Wolf, who was the first person to hear anything about "a cookbook" and not laugh.

R·I·V·E·R·W·A·L·K

On August 28, 1986, along the banks of the Mississippi, Riverwalk was given to the city of New Orleans. With over 200 shops, restaurants and cafes, it has brought life back to the waterfront. As part of the celebration of its opening, the "Legends of Louisiana" library was created. It is a collection of stories about famous and infamous people peppered with historic vignettes of river folk life. These legends are included in a permanent display at Riverwalk along with a "Food Wall of Fame," featuring recipes from local establishments and individuals.

Exactly one year later, *The Legends of Louisiana Cookbook* has evolved. It is a tribute to New Orleans' fine cuisine and colorful history. . .a continuing blend of recipes and stories handed down through generations and practiced by today's "living legends."

Chapter I
...some History

In order to better understand how New Orleans cuisine evolved, it is imperative to know a little about the history of the land, its resources and the people who use it. The legends in this chapter introduce us to the Creoles, the Acadians, the Choctaws, the Africans and some individuals whose contributions have made an impact on that history. The recipes are, of course, included.

Evolution of New Orleans Cuisine

Submitted by Ella Brennan, Commander's Palace Restaurant

We're very fortunate in New Orleans. Local cuisine is something very special. We've known it for years, and the rest of the world is fast catching on finally.

We have seafood in New Orleans: fresh from the Gulf of Mexico, fresh from Lake Pontchartrain, fresh from the nearby lakes and bayous. We also have an abundance of produce grown in our midst: mirlitons, sweet potatoes, luscious tomatoes, eggplants and, of course, we have some of the finest beef, veal and pork.

Perhaps, though, what makes our local cuisine so special is what we do with our indigenous products when we get them in our kitchens. Again, we have a heritage that is rich and varied.

We had, in New Orleans, the French settlers. We had the blacks from Africa. We had the Spaniards. Over the early years of New Orleans history these divergent ethnic groups adapted their methods of cooking to the cornucopia of fresh products they found in their new surroundings and produced a local cuisine unequaled anywhere in the United States.

Creole, even Cajun, cookery is now the rage of the country. It is still best enjoyed, however, right here where it started.

Creole Stewed Tomatoes

Submitted by Linda Laudumiey, The Brass Lion

Creole people were the first to use tomatoes in cooking in New Orleans (only in June, July, and August when tomatoes were in high season). They became known as the creole tomatoes.

12 slices	bacon
1½ cups	chopped fresh ham
1½ cups	chopped onions
15 large	creole tomatoes
6 slices	bread toasted
	salt and pepper
	to taste
½ cup	bread crumbs

Fry bacon in large skillet and drain. Chop bacon in small pieces. Turn bacon grease on low heat and sauté ham and drain.

Sauté onions until tender, leave in skillet. Cut the tops off of tomatoes, spoon out pulp from inside, leaving thick shell and set tomatoes aside. In large bowl chop up tomato pulp in bite-size pieces and combine with bite-size pieces of toasted bread. Add bacon and ham pieces to mixture and blend together. Salt and pepper to taste. Put tomato mixture in large skillet and combine with onions and drippings. Cook 15 to 20 minutes on medium low heat. Add bread crumbs to mixture after 5 minutes, add more salt and pepper to taste. Stir often until mixture starts sticking to pan and becomes creamy. When cool put mixture in shells, sprinkle top with bread crumbs. Bake at 350°, uncovered, for about 15 to 20 minutes. **Variation:** When tomatoes are not in season, 2 cans (28 ounces each) whole peeled tomatoes may be substituted. **Serves:** 6-8

Creole

Submitted By Merrill Barthe

Creole is a term used originally to denote persons born in the West Indies of Spanish parents, as distinguished from immigrants from Spain, Blacks, and Indians. In the United States the term is used chiefly to designate the French-speaking descendants of the early French and Spanish settlers in Louisiana.

Court of Two Sisters
Shrimp Creole

Submitted by The Court of Two Sisters Restaurant

¼ pound	butter
1 cup	chopped green peppers
1 cup	chopped onions
1 cup	diced celery
1 cup	diced shallots
2 cups	chopped canned tomatoes
1 cup	tomato pureé or two Tablespoons tomato paste
2	bay leaves
3 pounds	peeled deveined shrimp
2 ounces	cornstarch
1 pint	cold water
1 ounce	lemon juice
	salt
	pepper
	cayenne

Melt butter, sauté peppers, onions, celery, shallots for 5 minutes. Add tomato pureé or paste, bay leaves, and simmer 15 minutes. Add shrimp and simmer 15 minutes; dissolve cornstarch in 1 pint cold water, add and simmer 5 minutes. Add lemon juice, salt and pepper to taste; add pinch of cayenne, simmer 15 minutes. Serve over steamed rice or creamed potatoes. **Serves: 8**

Baked Stuffed Mirliton

Submitted by Mrs. Fernand Laudumiey, Jr.

Mirliton: this perhaps unfamiliar vegetable grows on trellised vines in New Orleans, and is a member of the gourd family. It has a mild flavor and cooks like squash. Other names for it are chayote, christophene, and vegetable pear. Eggplant may be substituted.

10 mirlitons,	halved and parboiled
¼ cup	corn oil
1 large	onion, chopped
4 or 5	green onions, chopped
1½ pounds	medium peeled shrimp
4 or 5 slices	stale or toasted white bread, broken into pieces
	salt and pepper to taste
¼ cup	parsley or 2 Tablespoons dried parsley
	butter or oleo
	cracker crumbs or bread crumbs

Parboil mirlitons till tender, take out seeds and scoop out pulp leaving about ⅛″ around skin. (This can be done a day or two ahead.) Do not remove juice. Put corn oil in large frying pan or dutch oven. When hot, add onions and green onions (shallots). Cook until wilted. Add chopped raw shrimp and cook until pink. Add mirliton pulp which has been combined with bread. (If bread is real stale, put in cold water and squeeze.) Cook and stir often, chopping the mirliton and bread mixture to incorporate, until it reaches a creamy consistency on medium low fire at least 30 minutes. Salt and pepper to taste. Add parsley. When cool, put mixture in mirliton shells, sprinkle with cracker crumbs or plain bread crumbs. Bake in 350° oven 20 to 25 minutes.

This recipe may be frozen. Bake in frozen state (do not defrost) for 45 minutes (30 minutes covered, 15 minutes uncovered). **Hint:** During cooking period if mixture sticks to pan, add butter or oleo, not oil. **Variations:** If skins are undesirable, mixture may be put into casserole. This recipe can be used for eggplant, and also white squash.

Eat with rice and enjoy. **Serves:** 6-8

Daube Glacé Creole

Submitted by Mrs. St. Denis J. Villere

5 pounds	veal round
½ pound	salt pork
	salt and pepper
1 teaspoon	whole cloves
	vinegar
1 large	onion, chopped fine
2	carrots chopped fine
1 quart	water
½	hog's head
3	pig's feet
4	veal knuckles
2 stalks	celery
1	lemon
2 pods	garlic
	bay leaves
	thyme
2 cups	sherry

Lard veal with salt pork, rub with salt and pepper, and pierce both sides with cloves. Cover with vinegar and let stand overnight. Remove meat from vinegar. Brown meat on both sides in a heavy pot. Add onion and carrots (both chopped fine) and simmer for 10 minutes. Add a quart of water and the vinegar. Cover and cook about 3 hours, until the meat falls from the bone. Remove veal from liquor. In a separate pot, place hog's head and all other ingredients. Cover with water and cook until they fall to pieces. Strain and add sherry. Pour over daube, and let jell overnight.

Daube Froide (Cold Daube)

Courtesy of Riverwalk

A great wintertime favorite of Louisiana Creoles was daube froide, or cold daube, sometimes also called daube glacé. In cold enough weather it was even sometimes sold by street vendors. Now it is rarely seen on restaurant menus, but is sometimes cooked at home. Here is a recipe adapted to modern tastes, ingredients, and methods of preparation.

3 pounds	beef round
3 Tablespoons	olive oil
1 Tablespoon	flour
1 medium	onion, chopped
1½ large	shallots, chopped
1 can (6 ounces)	Italian-style tomato paste
1 cup	boiling water
3 ribs	celery, chopped
1	bay leaf
3	cloves garlic, minced
2 Tablespoons	salt
½ teaspoon	cayenne or black pepper
½ of 3 ounce	envelope gelatin
½ cup	water
2 medium	whole boiled carrots lettuce

Trim the beef round, removing fat and gristle. Rinse and pat dry. Sauté in olive oil in a heavy cast-iron pot until the meat is tender, about 1 hour. Turn occasionally in order to prevent burning. Shred the cooked meat into stringy "fingers" by picking it with a fork.

Prepare a roux by browning 1 tablespoon flour in the pan drippings and a little more oil if necessary. Add onion and shallots, stir and sauté until brown. Add tomato paste and boiling water, celery, a bay leaf, and garlic. Cook until flavors are somewhat blended and then put the meat back into the pot

16

with other ingredients. Fill the pot to the brim with more water, add salt, cayenne or black pepper, and simmer gently on low heat for about 2 hours.

After this cooking process, more than a quart of liquid should remain. Dissolve gelatin in water and add to the gravy. Place carrots lengthwise in the bottom of the dish in which you intend to mold the daube. Pour the gravy and meat into the dish. Chill for several hours and serve on fresh lettuce leaves on a large platter. Slice. An ideal party or special supper dish reminiscent of old Creole days. **Serves:** 6-8

Delmonico Baked Creole Eggplant

Submitted by Delmonico Restaurant

2	eggplants, peeled and diced
1 medium	onion, chopped
2 stalks	celery, chopped
1 cup	small shrimp
1	tomato, chopped
	dash Tabasco®
	dash Lea & Perrins®
1	bay leaf
¼ cup	seasoned bread crumbs
	butter or oil for sautéeing

Parboil eggplant. Sauté onion, celery, and shrimp in butter or oil. Add tomato and cook. Add seasoning. When all are melted and blended together, fold in eggplant. Place in baking dish, top with seasoned bread crumbs, and bake in oven set at 350° for approximately 20 minutes. **Serves:** 4

New Orleans' Famous French Market—Meats and Vegetables

Courtesy of Riverwalk

Since French colonial times, produce, meat, poultry, and seafood have been brought to New Orleans in boats that docked along the Mississippi riverbank in front of the Place d'Armes. This spot was once the army parade grounds at the center of the town, and is known today as Jackson Square. At this convenient location, merchandise was bought and sold. Later, to facilitate trade, buildings were erected to house the meat purveyors, vegetable vendors, and merchants of other commodities. Soon came an assortment of colorful canopies, stalls, and blankets on the ground to display the goods and refreshments of every description. It was an exciting, noisy, fragrant, and bustling marketplace! Although the purpose and look of the French Market has changed over the years, it stands as a monument and constant reminder of New Orleans' rich mercantile past.

Veal Francesca

Submitted by Anthony DiPiazza, Chef Du Maison, Pascal's Manale Restaurant

2 pieces (4 ounces each)	veal
2 ounces	noodles
1 cup	red sauce
3 slices	eggplant
2 ounces	parmesan cheese
2 slices	mozzarella cheese

In a sauce pan sauté veal. Remove from flame. Boil noodles until done and drain. Place noodles on the bottom of a casserole dish. Place veal on top of noodles and add the red sauce. Place the eggplant with parmesan cheese sprinkled on top. Then cover with mozzarella cheese. Bake at 350° until brown and serve. **Serves: 2**

Cream of Leek Chantilly

Submitted by The Versailles Restaurant

3 or 4 medium size	leeks (white part only, finely chopped and well washed)
1 Tablespoon	garlic, minced
4 Tablespoons	fresh butter
5 Tablespoons	all purpose flour
5 cups	stock from leek trimmings
2 cubes	chicken boullion
2	bay leaves
½ cup	heavy cream
	salt, white pepper, to taste
1 cup	fresh whipped cream

Stew leeks and garlic gently in butter until they begin to turn clear. Add flour, stirring constantly. Cook roux 10 minutes (do not brown). Add stock in three stages, mixing thoroughly each time. Add bouillon cubes and bay leaf and simmer gently 25-30 minutes. Add heavy cream with salt and pepper to taste and simmer 10 more minutes.

To serve, ladle boiling soup into hot cups or bowls. Garnish each serving with a dollop of freshly whipped cream. **Serves:** 4

Pot au Feu
(Soup Meat, to You)

Courtesy of Riverwalk

One of the many things that the French and New Orleans Creoles have in common is soup meat, or Pot au Feu, as the French call it. In New Orleans, it was traditionally served on Saturdays, following some popular entertainment.

The French serve the elements of Pot au Feu meat, vegetables, and soup separately. They dunk the meat in coarse or cooking salt. The Creoles, equipped with palates trained to sharper tastes, prefer a dip of horseradish, Creole mustard (coarse ground), and ketchup or mayonnaise; the proportions of each varying according to individual taste. You're on your own in mixing up the dip to suit your tastes. But here's a recipe for the soup meat:

Place the brisket in cold water. Turn the heat up high. When the water boils, skim off all the film that develops on top. Add a teaspoon of salt. Simmer at a half boil until the meat is tender, about an hour. Add cleaned carrots, turnips, cabbage, celery, potatoes, and such, along with some thyme, black pepper, two bay leaves, and a few sprigs of parsley. Some hot sausage or pickled pork also may be added. Continue to simmer until the vegetables are cooked to the degree of doneness that you prefer.

Tabasco® or Louisiana hot sauce are also good accompaniments.

New Orleans' Famous French Market—Fish

Courtesy of Riverwalk

Visitors to the French Market in the late nineteenth century remarked on the riot of color and activity. They spoke of "great tubs of moving crabs, huge piles of shrimp and jackfish, redfish, reel trout, bluefish, red snapper, flounders, croakers and mullets." One found buyers and vendors hawking their wares in the crowded marketplace; the bartering and bargaining being shouted in a profusion of Spanish, French, English, and German. Added to this were the sounds of chickens, parrots and other caged birds; live alligators, cure-all salesmen, and even dentists, who for a few picayunes would pull your bad teeth right in the center of the market building, for all to see.

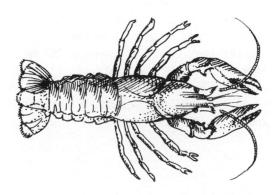

Oysters Commander

Submitted by Commander's Palace Restaurant

To prepare the stuffing:

4 Tablespoons	flour
4 Tablespoons	butter

Prepare a blond roux and set aside:

40	oysters
2 cups	green onions, chopped
1 medium	onion, minced
1 clove	garlic, minced
12	artichoke bottoms
2 cups	oyster liquor
2	bay leaves
¼ teaspoon	Seafood Seasoning salt and pepper to taste

Grind the oysters, green onion, white onion, garlic and artichoke bottoms.

Bring oyster liquor to a boil. Add the above mixture, the bay leaves, Seafood Seasoning, salt and pepper. Simmer for 10-15 minutes. Now add the roux and stir until it is well blended. Reduce the heat. Simmer on a low fire, stirring constantly until the mixture is very thick. Set aside until cool, and then refrigerate until ready for serving.

Sauce for Oysters Commander:

4 Tablespoons	butter
4 Tablespoons	flour

Prepare a blond roux:

24	oysters
2 cups	oyster liquor
2	bay leaves
¼ teaspoon	Seafood Seasoning
2 cups	scallions, coarsely chopped
1 cup	artichoke hearts, quartered
	salt and pepper to taste
	artichoke leaves
	parsley for garnish

In a sauté pan place the oysters, oyster liquor, bay leaves and Seafood Seasoning. Poach the oysters until the edges curl. Remove the oysters. Set aside.

Reduce the oyster liquor to 1½ cups. To this, add the roux, and stir until well blended. Add the scallions and the artichoke hearts; adjust the salt and pepper. Return the oysters to this sauce and keep warm.

To serve, place one oyster on each artichoke bottom. Put stuffing in a pastry bag with star tip. Squeeze the stuffing in a mound on artichoke bottom. Bake in a 425° oven for 15 minutes or until golden. Ladle the Oysters Commander Sauce over this, and garnish with 4 large outside artichoke leaves and a sprig of fresh parsley. **Serves: 4**

Seafood Terrine

Submitted by Broussard's Restaurant

4 ounces	butter
1 pound	shrimp
1 medium	onion, minced
2 cloves	garlic minced
2 Tablespoons	green peppercorn
¼ cup	brandy
1 pound	redfish
1 pound	trout
1 pound	crabmeat
1 bunch	parsley, chopped
1 bunch	fresh dill, chopped
¼ cup	lemon juice
¼ cup	gin
	salt and white pepper to taste
1 pint	whipping cream

In a 10-inch sauté pan, add butter and sauté shrimp, onion, garlic and peppercorns. Flambé with brandy. Let cool in freezer until semi-frozen. Place remaining ingredients (except whipping cream) into meat grinder and, at the end, slowly incorporate whipping cream. Then add sautéed mixture and fold in. Place mixture into buttered mold, cover with aluminum foil and bake in water bath (bain marie) at 400° for 40 minutes. Refrigerate overnight. Slice into desired thickness and lace with fresh dill sauce.

Dill Sauce:

4 cups	vegetable oil
5	whole eggs
2 cups	prepared mustard
1 cup	sugar
1 cup	white vinegar
1 Tablespoon	Worcestershire sauce
1 bunch	dill, finely chopped

Blend ingredients, except dill, in mixer on low speed for 2 minutes, slowly adding vegetable oil until you achieve a smooth consistency. Add chopped dill. Spoon small amount over terrine.
Serves: 10

Trout Marguery

Submitted by Chiqui Collier, Cookery N'Orleans Style Restaurant

4 fillets (6-8 ounces each)	**trout**
	salt and lemon pepper to taste
3 Tablespoons	**olive oil**
2	**egg yolks**
2 sticks	**butter, melted**
1 Tablespoon	**fresh lemon juice**
1 cup	**cooked shrimp, chopped**
½ pound	**lump crabmeat**
½ cup	**sliced mushrooms, sautéed in butter**
¼ cup	**dry white wine**
	paprika

Place trout fillets in a 2 quart Pyrex® dish. Season with a little salt and lemon pepper. Drizzle with olive oil. Bake at 375° for 25 minutes. Meanwhile, place egg yolks in top of a double boiler (over hot, not boiling water). Gradually beat in melted butter, stir until thickened. Stir in lemon juice. Gently fold in remaining ingredients. Cook, stirring over low heat for about 15 minutes in double boiler. Pour over fish. Run under broiler to brown lightly.
Serves: 4

New Orleans' Famous French Market—Coffee

Courtesy of Riverwalk

Coffee stands have long been a tradition at the French Market. New Orleanians would flock to the market after church or the opera to savor the delicious Creole café au lait or café noir. This remains so today, even though most of the market has been enclosed to form air conditioned shops.

Café Brûlot

Submitted by Antoine's

2 sticks	cinnamon
8	cloves
1 peel	of a lemon
2 Tablespoons	sugar
3 ounces	brandy
3 cups	strong coffee (hot)

Heat all ingredients, except the coffee, in a pot for a few minutes while stirring. Pour in hot coffee and serve. Use additional sugar to taste. **Hint:** At the restaurant, we heat the cinnamon, cloves, lemon peel, sugar, and brandy in a heavy copper bowl and flame it at the table. The flame is doused with the hot coffee and served into cups specially designed for Café Brûlot at Antoine's. **Serves: 3**

Choctaw Contributions to Creole Cuisine

Courtesy of Riverwalk

When the Europeans and Africans arrived in Louisiana, the Choctaws were here. They introduced the newcomers to sagamite (grits) and to one of the most widely used spices for that local favorite, gumbo. Tradition claims that the present site of Decatur and North Peters was the trading post used by the Indians and that they brought baskets of herbs and sassafras leaves to trade. Filé is made from dried sassafras leaves compounded to a powder. The Choctaws were friendly to the white men and would come to sell their wares. On Sunday they would gather in front of the St. Louis Cathedral with basketry, beads, pottery and filé. There, shoppers would avail themselves of the opportunity to purchase the necessary items needed for their gumbo, which has developed into a dish widely associated with New Orleans.

Gumbo Filé

Submitted by Mrs. Thomas Airey Parker

1 large (5 pounds)	tender chicken, cut into pieces
	salt and pepper
	cayenne to taste
2 Tablespoons	butter or 1 Tablespoon lard
3 Tablespoons	flour
1 large	onion, diced
3 sprigs	parsley
1 sprig	thyme
2 large	slices or ½ pound lean ham, diced
2 quarts	boiling water
2 quarts	oyster water
1	bay leaf
½ pod	red pepper (without seed)
3 dozen	oysters
2 teaspoons	filé

Sprinkle chicken well with salt and pepper, and cayenne to taste. Fry slowly in fat in a large pot until brown. When chicken is brown, pour off shortening, leaving about two tablespoons in the bottom of utensil. Add flour and stir until a brown roux is made, then add onion, parsley, thyme and, when nicely brown, add ham, chicken, boiling water and oyster stock (which has been previously heated). Add bay leaf, pepper pod and simmer for an hour longer. When ready to serve, add fresh oysters. Let gumbo cook three minutes longer. Remove from fire and add filé, stirring slowly to mix thoroughly. Serve with boiled rice. **Serves:** 10-12

Creole Feast

Courtesy of Riverwalk

Louisiana had an abundance of resources to delight the tastes of its citizens, and these were used to develop the exquisite cuisine that was characteristic of an earlier age. The Creole breakfast, for example, was quite a feast. Black coffee would be taken in the morning; then at a later hour, the main breakfast would be served. It included several different meats and always grillades, grits, biscuits and pain perdu (lost bread), more commonly known as French toast

Pain Perdu (Lost Bread)

Submitted by Austin Leslie, Chez Helene Restaurant

3 eggs	beaten
½ cup	milk
½ cup	sugar
2 Tablespoons	orange flower water
1 Tablespoon	grated lemon zest
¼ cup	brandy
½ teaspoon	nutmeg
8 slices	stale French bread
2 Tablespoons	butter
2 Tablespoons	vegetable oil
	powdered sugar
	cane syrup

Combine eggs, milk, sugar, orange flower water, lemon zest, brandy and nutmeg in bowl. Mix well. Soak bread in liquid mixture. Heat butter and oil in heavy frying pan. Fry bread until golden brown. Dust with powdered sugar and serve with warm cane syrup. **Serves:** 4

Homemade Biscuits

Submitted by Betty Comeaux

2 cups	unbleached white flour
1 Tablespoon	baking powder
2 teaspoons	sugar
1 teaspoon	salt
⅓ cup	shortening
⅔ cup	milk

Mix flour, baking powder, sugar and salt with electric hand mixer. Blend in shortening. Mix in milk with a fork. Knead about 12-15 strokes. Pat out on floured surface ½-inch to ¾-inch thick. Cut and bake on ungreased cookie sheet at 450° for 10-12 minutes. **Yield:** approximately 16 biscuits

French Toast

Submitted by Mary Michael

3	eggs
3 Tablespoons	cream
1 loaf	French bread, cut into 1-inch slices
2 Tablespoons	butter
	cinnamon
	honey

Beat eggs and cream. Dip bread in mixture. Melt butter in skillet. Place bread in buttered skillet and sprinkle with cinnamon. Cook until golden brown and turn. Serve with honey. **Serves:** 4

Waste Not—Want Not

Submitted by Emelyn McCue

New Orleans is unique in its diversity of people and their various backgrounds, customs, legends, and cuisine. The one common thread is the warmth and friendliness of its people, namely, Southern Hospitality. True "natives" will welcome you into their homes, serve you a cup of coffee and feed you some of the best food in the world!

Many of the "Southern", "Nawlin's" and "Cajun" dishes have been derived from the "Waste Not—Want Not" message, which has been handed down from generation to generation.

When you had "drop-in" company, Mama went to the old ice box (refrigerator before electricity) and the cupboard to see what was on hand. She would put it all together and cook up a fantastic tasting dish. Never a recipe, just put-it-all-together-and-serve. If any of this was left, it was put into the ice box to possibly use again in the same manner.

For example, when breakfast was prepared, there were "always" grits, and plenty of them. Of course there were some left over, so "Waste Not—Want Not!" Fried Grits came to be. Another breakfast treat from yesterday's leftover bread (Pain Perdu, or "lost bread") is French toast.

Fried Grits

Courtesy of Riverwalk

1 cup	leftover cooked grits (or prepare 1 cup as directed on package)
2	eggs beaten
	salt and pepper to taste
¼ to ⅓ cup	vegetable oil
	butter

If preparing grits from package, when the grits are cooked, set aside to cool slightly (10-15 minutes), then pour into a shallow platter or baking dish. They should be the thickness of fudge, ½-inch to ¾-inch. Cover grits with waxed paper then place in refrigerator for several hours or overnight. To prepare the grits for frying, cut into 2-inch squares.

Beat eggs with salt and pepper to taste. Put oil in fry pan and heat on medium-high heat. Oil should be hot when grits are placed into pan. Dip each 2-inch square into egg mixture and place immediately into oil. Fry only long enough to lightly brown the egg coating, turn for just about one minute, remove from pan onto paper towel to drain. Place small pat of butter on each square, serve and enjoy. **Serves:** 4

Couche-Couche a Dejeuner (Cush-Cush at Breakfast)

Courtesy of Riverwalk

Older Louisianians fondly remember a rich and savory cornmeal mush served to them on cold winter mornings when they were little children. Found throughout the South under various names, such as cush-cush, cuz-cuz, and coush-coush, it was known in Southern Louisiana as couche-couche. Stemming from the Arab cous-cous, a combination of cooked grain, meat and vegetables, it traveled to the French colony of Louisiana with African slaves, who adapted their ration of cornmeal to their taste and introduced it to the French colonists. It is reportedly found as far south as Brazil, where it has the same name and the same history down there.

Other variants on the expression include couche-couche caillé (pronounced "koosh-koosh-KEYE"), the name for the dish when served with milk, clabber, or buttermilk. The expression has also taken on the meaning of light kissing or lovemaking and of unearned money, such as you might get from Auntie Vera on your Saint's Day—a sort of wonderful windfall.

The recipe is simple, the variations endless:

2 cups	cornmeal
1 Tablespoon	baking powder
½ cup	sugar
2 cups	milk
2	eggs
¼ cup	melted butter

Mix together cornmeal, baking powder and sugar. In a separate bowl mix milk, eggs and melted butter. Add wet ingredients to dry and pour batter into a greased skillet or pot on the stove. As it cooks against the side of the pot, scrape toward the center. Repeat five or six times until all the batter is cooked to the consistency of spoonbread.

No two recipes, however, are identical. Some people grease the skillet liberally with hot bacon, ham, or sausage drippings. Some serve the mush with cane syrup or blackstrap molasses. When green onions were available, another kind of couche-couche developed, to be eaten with meat or fish. This last onion-flavored couche-couche, picking up celery, sage, eggs, chicken broth, and other good things as the dish moved toward the eastern part of the South became very like (and may have been the ancestor of) the familiar cornbread dressing now so often served with baked chicken or turkey.

A rather humble dish, couche-couche ultimately evolved far from its origins as a southern Louisiana breakfast food. Yet it remained popular in its original form among those humble, French-speaking people who were wont to declare, "Les pauvres gens vous donnent a dejeuner dans leurs coeurs. (Poor people give breakfast with their hearts.)"

Couche-Couche

Submitted by Eunice F. V. Dedebant

"Adieu les mariés, couche-couche et caillé" is a saying called out to honeymooners. Literally it means: "Goodby newlyweds, couche-couche clabber." It is meant to remind them that although today it is wedding cakes and wine, tomorrow it will be back to the everyday fare of couche-couche and clabber again.

Couche-couche is a cereal eaten with either milk or café au lait. It can also take the place of bread or rice in dressings.

2 cups	cornmeal (preferably yellow)
1½ teaspoons	salt
1 teaspoon	baking powder
1½ cup	milk or water
¼ cup	lard, melted and heated hot

Use a heavy iron pot or skillet. Mix the first four ingredients thoroughly and put into the heated shortening. Let a crust form. Give a good stir and lower the flame to simmer. Cover and cook 15 minutes, stirring occasionally. **Serves:** 6

The First Cooking School

Submitted by Mel Leavitt, Historian, Author and TV Commentator

The first cooking school in America was established in New Orleans in 1722. The young ladies who had come to this swampy wilderness to marry settlers were unhappy. They were good cooks, but unfamiliar with such products as corn and grits. Anyway, they preferred wheat bread, which was scarce if not nonexistent.

Governor Bienville's housekeeper, Madame Langlois, pacified them by organizing a cooking school. This was 4 years after New Orleans was founded. . .before the City had been built or fortified.

Madame Langlois taught the ladies how to grind maize to make cornmeal, how to make hominy grits and how to combine butter beans and corn into succotash.

Sidney's Cornbread

Submitted by Austin Leslie, Chez Helene Restaurant

½ cup	sifted flour
1½ cups	yellow corn meal
1 teaspoon	salt
2 teaspoons	sugar
3 teaspoons	baking powder
3	eggs, beaten lightly
1 cup	milk
¼ cup	cream
½ cup	butter, melted

Sift dry ingredients together in bowl. Add eggs and milk and beat with spoon until mixture is just moist. Beat in cream and melted butter. (Do not overbeat.) Pour batter into 8½ × 11-inch buttered pan. Bake at 400° for 15 to 20 minutes.
Yield: approximately 12 pieces

Corn Fritters

Submitted by the Alcée-Hymel Family

1 cup	sifted flour
1 teaspoon	baking powder
½ teaspoon	salt
¼ teaspoon	sugar
1	egg, slightly beaten
4 Tablespoons	melted shortening
½ cup	milk
2 cups	whole kernel corn, drained
	oil for deep frying
	maple or cane syrup

Mix and sift flour, baking powder, salt and sugar. Beat egg, melted shortening and milk together with rotary egg beater. Add corn, and combine with dry ingredients, mixing well. Drop by spoonfuls into deep boil (365°) for 3 to 5 minutes, or until golden brown. Drain on paper. Serve hot as vegetable, or with maple or cane syrup. **Yield:** 12-15 fritters

Grillades & Grits

Submitted by Austin Leslie, Chez Helene Restaurant

8 slices (4 ounces each)	veal
¼ cup	flour
¼ cup	bacon drippings
1 cup	onions, chopped
½ cup	celery, chopped
½ cup	green pepper, chopped
2 toes	garlic, finely chopped
1	bay leaf
½ teaspoon	thyme
1 teaspoon	Lea & Perrins® Worcestershire sauce
1 can (16 ounces)	whole tomatoes, crushed
1 can (8 ounces)	tomato sauce
1 cup	beef stock or water (hot)
¼ teaspoon	cayenne pepper
¼ cup	parsley, finely chopped
¼ cup	green onions, finely chopped salt and pepper to taste flour (for dusting) butter

Salt and pepper veal slices, dust in flour and brown in butter. Set aside. Combine flour and bacon drippings over moderate heat and stir constantly until brown. Add onions, celery, pepper, garlic and sauté gently for 5 minutes. Next, add all other ingredients, except parsely and green onions. Stir sauce and simmer ½ hour. Return veal slices to sauce and simmer until tender. Add chopped parsley and green onions and serve over freshly cooked grits. **Serves:** 4

The Herb Garden

Submitted by Mel Leavitt, Historian, Author and TV Commentator

Anyone not native-born and bred is apt to be amazed at the number of herbs and spices used in a New Orleans kitchen. In fact, when the Ursuline nuns first arrived in 1730, a special treaty was signed guaranteeing them sufficient ground to make a garden...an herb garden. It was planted by Sister Xavier who compounded the medicines for the Royal hospital. She became the first woman pharmacist in the New World. There was bay leaf for sprains, marjoram for convulsions and dropsy. Oregano helped rheumatism. Dill induced a sound sleep.

The herb garden entered into every aspect of Creole life. It provided innumerable beverages. Tea could be made with mint or bay leaf or even dandelions. Liqueurs were developed from anisette, citronelle and absinthe. Spruce beer was considered quite good. Chevril was used to make vinegar, and coriander seed to flavor pastry. To these, the settlers added local specialties. Filé (today a gumbo staple) was made by the Choctaw Indians from dried and powdered sassafras leaves. Herbs were added bountifully to courtbouillon, bouillabaisse and jambalaya. The Old Ursulines cookbook notes that, in fact, "few truly Creole dishes can be prepared without some variant of herb bouquet to accentuate flavor and bring out the special delicacy of the central ingredient."

At one time, almost every New Orleans household had its own herb garden...gathered at the height of growth...washed, tied in bundles to dry and later put into dark bottles for storage. No cuisine on earth utilizes more or better herbs or spices, and it all is a legacy of Sister Xavier and her first herb garden planted 260 years ago for medicinal purposes.

Courtbouillon

Submitted by Lillie Petit Gallagher, "Oilfield Journal"

	basic roux (see below)
1 can (29 ounces)	tomato sauce
2 cans (6 ounces each)	tomato paste
6 pounds	fish, preferably channel bass or red snapper, cut in pieces

Cook roux with tomato sauce and paste thoroughly, then add fish and cook slowly until done, stirring very gently in order not to break up fish pieces. Serve with rice.

Basic Roux:

5 Tablespoons	fat (vegetable oil or smoked bacon fat)
1 rounded Tablespoon	flour (for thicker sauce make roux with 2-4 Tablespoons flour instead of 1)
2 pounds	onions, chopped fine
3 pieces	celery, chopped fine
1 medium	bell pepper, chopped fine
1	lemon (use grated rind, then remove white pulpy membrane and chop rest of lemon)
3 pods	garlic
few dashes	each of Worcestershire sauce, Tabasco®, thyme; McCormick Season All®
2	bay leaves
	salt to taste

To the fat, add flour and brown, stirring constantly. Add the onions, fry slowly until well browned and reduced to pulp. Add the rest of the ingredients and continue to cook slowly for at least 30 to 45 minutes. **Serves:** 12-16

Bouillabaisse

Courtesy of Riverwalk

4 medium	carrots, sliced
2	onions, sliced
6 stalks	celery, sliced
2	leeks (white parts only), sliced
2	fennel roots (if available), sliced
½ stick	butter
2 Tablespoons	tomato paste
1 cup	brandy
2 cups	white wine
3	fresh tomatoes, seeded and peeled
½ teaspoon	garlic, finely chopped
pinch	presoaked saffron
3 quarts	fish broth
1 pound	shrimp
1 pound	skinless, boneless fish fillets (cut into 1-inch pieces)
½ dozen	freshly shucked oysters
6 medium	lobster tail meat
6	mussels in shell
¾ cup	fresh lump crabmeat
	chopped parsley
	garlic croutons

Sauté sliced vegetables in butter until glazy looking. Add tomato paste, sauté, and flame with brandy. Extinguish flame with white wine. Add tomatoes, garlic and saffron. Add fish broth. Cook until vegetables are done.

In large pot, separately sauté in butter, shrimp, fish, oysters, lobster tail meat, and mussels in shell.

Add fish broth to pot containing seafood. Cook

until fish is done, approximately 15-20 minutes. Reduce heat, cook for 10 minutes. Correct seasoning and wine to taste. Top with fresh lump crabmeat and chopped parsley. Serve garlic croutons with soup. **Serves:** 6

Le Filet De Lapin A La Moutarde (Rabbit with Creole Mustard Sauce)

Submitted by Chef Michel Marcais, La Fête 1984

6 filets	rabbit
1 cup	white wine
1 pinch	thyme
2	bay leaves
2 Tablespoons	oil
3 Tablespoons	Creole mustard
1 cup	heavy cream
	salt and pepper to taste

Marinate rabbit filets with ½ cup wine, thyme and bay leaves for 24 hours.

Sauté rabbit in oil lightly, then remove rabbit. Add remaining wine and creole mustard and simmer for 5 minutes. Remove from heat and blend in cream and salt and pepper to taste.

Slice rabbit lenghwise in strips. Place sauce over rabbit and serve. **Serves:** 6

Cajun Cuisine—A Living Symbol of the People Who Prepare It

Submitted by John D. Folse, Lafitte's Landing

Cajun food reflects a way of life. Usually hot and spicy, the food is a toast to the good life and the land that Cajuns have come to love in South Louisiana. Like gumbo, Cajun cooking is unpretentious yet exotic in flavor. It takes and adapts whatever is at hand and blends it into taste tempting dishes. It is rich in variety. Cajun cooking is an unending delight which captures the taste of the most skeptical of newcomers, and seduces them into the local lifestyle.

The Cajuns—a corruption of the word Acadian—are descendants of French Colonists exiled from Nova Scotia in 1753. After years of wandering and searching for a land where they could reconstruct the lifestyle they had enjoyed in Acadia, as their homeland was then known, they came to Louisiana.

The land that welcomed the Acadians is Bayou country. Swamp and bayou have played important roles in shaping the Louisiana Cajun's unique identity and culinary tradition. Through bountiful gifts of seafood and wildlife, the land encourages the creation of a cuisine unlike any other in the world.

Cajun cooking reflects both the affluence of the geographic locale and its French flavored legacy. Bayou and gulf waters are teeming with shrimp, crabs, oysters, and a rich variety of fish. In the winter the marshes and lakes attract thousands of ducks and geese flying south from Canada. Even the swamp, once dark and mysterious, produces crawfish, catfish, and frogs' legs in abundance. The land along the banks of the bayous and rivers is rich in its yield of okra, eggplant, peppers, yams, rice, tomatoes, squash and countless other vegetables.

These were the ingredients which served as raw materials for Cajun cuisine.

When the Acadians first began settling the area, there was no social contact. They were tied to the land and had to be rugged and adaptable. For them, life was a day to day, season to season struggle to sustain their families and their culture. Their meals more than likely came out of one pot, one dish which combined all the blessings of life in South Louisiana such as fish, rice, spices, shellfish and abundant vegetables. Jambalaya, gumbo, sauce piquant, and crawfish étouffée stand as delicious examples of Cajun onepot meals.

Cajun cuisine is a living thing. It is a part of the people who prepare it. It is the love of food and family, a custom and a lifestyle. It is centuries of adaptive creation passed lovingly from mother to daughter, father to son, and friend to friend. It reflects a sensory pleasure and a "let's take life as it comes" attitude. These cultural and environmental ingredients and the people who have come to love them keep Cajun cooking alive in South Louisiana.

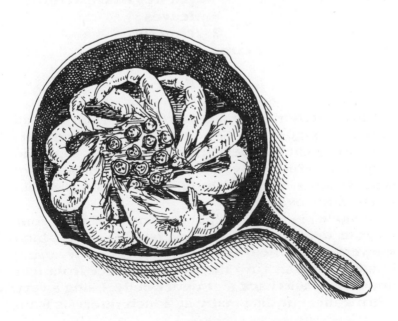

Cajun Cochon Du Lait (Suckling Pig)

Submitted by John D. Folse, Lafitte's Landing

1 large	suckling pig approximately 6-8 weeks old
	salt and pepper
	granulated garlic
	sage
	rosemary
	stuffing (your favorite recipe)
	butter
4 large	quartered onions
3 whole	garlic heads, sliced in half
1 bunch	celery
6	apples
	oven browned potatoes
	carrots
	parsley or fresh mint leaves
2	cherries
2 cups	red wine
	butter
	flour

Have butcher clean pig thoroughly, removing all entrails, tongue, etc. Season pig (inside and out) well using salt, pepper, granulated garlic, sage and a bit of rosemary. Overseason due to thickness of skin. Wrap the pig in aluminum foil and place in refrigerator overnight.

Remove pig from refrigerator and stuff with your favorite dressing. Do not overstuff. Using 4-inch skewers, truss belly cavity tying securely, using butcher's twine. Turn the pig over, place front feet under head and back feet under belly. Using a very sharp knife, cut diagonally at 2-inch intervals from head to tail, making cuts approximately ¼-inch deep. Make one incision from back of neck to top of tail along backbone. These cuts will enhance cooking and carving, and will allow fat to escape and baste pig during cooking.

Place the large end of a carrot or a small block of wood in the pig's mouth to keep open during cooking (to permit garnishing later). Place the pig feet down in roasting pan, brush lightly with butter. Wrap ears and tail in aluminum foil to prevent burning. Place 4 large quartered onions, 3 whole garlic heads, sliced in half (peelings need not be removed), 1 bunch of celery, 6 apples, halved, in the bottom of roasting pan. Place the pig in a preheated 350° oven, basting every 30-45 minutes with natural drippings and cook approximately 20 minutes per pound. When internal temperature reaches 170°F or 75°C and the skin is browned and crisp the cochon du lait is ready for serving.

Place the pig on a large carving board and reserve all pan juices. Garnish with oven browned potatoes and carrots, parsley or fresh mint leaves. Place a cherry in each eye and an apple in its mouth. To carve remove rear ham and front leg first. Slice all meat from these pieces. Insert carving knife in slit along backbone and remove loins, slice accordingly.

Take roasting pan with reserved juices, tilt and skim off excess fat. Place pan on stove top on high and bring juices to a boil. Deglaze with 2 cups red wine. Scrape bottom of pan well. Once reduced thicken with blonde roux (equal parts butter and flour), season to taste and serve in a gravy boat.
Serves: 10

Cajun Shrimp Spaghetti

Courtesy of Riverwalk

¼ cup	cooking oil
3 large	onions, finely chopped
1 large	sweet pepper, finely chopped
1 stalk	celery, finely chopped
2 cans (12 ounces each)	tomato paste
1 can (15 ounces)	tomato sauce
1 can (1 pound)	whole tomatoes, chopped
2 teaspoons	sugar
2 pounds	raw shrimp, peeled
1 teaspoon	dried parsley
3	cloves garlic, minced
1 quart	hot water
1 Tablespoon	Worcestershire sauce
2 teaspoons	red hot sauce
	salt and pepper to taste
1 pound	#4 spaghetti (uncooked)

Heat oil in heavy pot. Stir in onion, pepper, celery and cook until onion is a light brown. Add tomato paste, tomato sauce, whole tomatoes and sugar. Simmer until oil reappears, stir frequently. Add shrimp, parsley and garlic and simmer for 20 minutes, stir frequently. Add hot water, Worcestershire sauce, hot sauce, salt and pepper to taste and cook on medium heat for 1 hour or until sauce is nice and thick.

Cook spaghetti according to package direction. Spoon sauce over spaghetti and eat with garlic bread. **Serves: 6**

Redfish Bon Ton

Submitted by Bon Ton Café

6	redfish fillets (8 ounces each)
	salt to taste
	black pepper to taste
	paprika to taste
3 sticks	butter
	juice of 2 lemons
½ cup	of water
1 teaspoon	flour
¾ pound	lump crabmeat (approximately 2 cups)
½ cup	white wine
½ cup	chopped parsley

Sprinkle both sides of the redfish fillets with salt, pepper and paprika.

Melt 2 sticks of butter in a large skillet. Slightly brown the butter. Place the seasoned redfish in the skillet belly side down, and cook for 2 minutes over medium heat. Add the lemon juice. Turn the fish over, and add the water, then flour and mix. Lightly sprinkle the fish again with paprika. Cover the fish, and cook 8-10 minutes. Remove the cover, and simmer for 2-3 minutes more until the fish is done, depending on thickness of fillets. Remove the fish from the skillet, and place the fillets on heated plates. Stir the sauce remaining in the skillet. If the butter separates, add a little more water to achieve a sauce. Place the crabmeat in another pan. Marinate it over low heat in 1 stick of butter and the white wine until hot.

Serve the redfish topped with crabmeat and chopped parsley. Spoon some of the butter sauce over each serving. **Serves:** 6

Blackened Crab Cakes

Submitted by Al Copeland, Copeland's of New Orleans

2 pounds	redfish
1 Tablespoon	garlic, minced
¼ pound	butter, room temperature
	juice of 1 lemon
1 pound	claw crabmeat
½	chopped green onion
	Prudhomme's Blackened Redfish Seasoning®
	melted butter
	lemon wedges

   In food processor, blend redfish, garlic, butter and lemon juice to a smooth paste. Transfer to large mixing bowl. Add crabmeat and green onions. Fold mixture until well blended. Form mixture into 4 ounce patties. Coat each side with Blackened Redfish Seasoning. Char in white-hot cast iron skillet. Melted butter may be ladled on top or served on the side with lemon wedge. **Yield:** 12 crab cakes

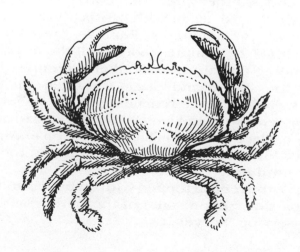

The Start of Amplified Music in Southwest Louisiana

Submitted by Luderine Darbone, Manager, Hackberry Ramblers

In the early days of Cajun music in southwest Louisiana, the soft sound of stringed instruments could not compete with the loud sound of accordion bands and orchestras at dance halls where large crowds congregated. The country dance halls were usually built to accommodate crowds of one hundred to two hundred couples and scores of onlookers. Cornmeal was distributed on the dance floor to make it slippery for easier dancing. As a result, when the music started, rubbing of shoe soles on the dance floor, together with the fun and excitement of the crowd, would make the music of a string band barely audible at a distance of twenty to thirty feet from the bandstand.

That was the situation when the Hackberry Ramblers of Hackberry, Louisiana organized their Cajun and Hillbilly string band in March, 1933. The type of music the band played was an immediate hit and demands for dance engagements started pouring in. The first dance by the Hackberry Ramblers in the Cajun country was played in Basile, Louisiana in May of 1933. Although the band was liked and larger crowds came at each engagement, there was something lacking because the music could not be heard in its fullness across the hall. With this in mind, Luderine Darbone, leader of the Hackberry Ramblers ordered an amplifying sound system in the fall of 1933 with the intention of using the amplification for voice and singing, not thinking the sound of the music would also be amplified. It was a happy day when the sound system, which consisted of a 20 Watt amplifier, one speaker, and one microphone, arrived and it was used for the first time. By placing the speaker on the wall opposite the bandstand, the crowds were able to hear the music as well as the singing throughout the dance hall. This made it much easier for the musicians to play a dance, and much easier for string bands to compete with the loud music of accordion and brass bands of that day.

The crowds at dance halls increased two-fold and other string bands immediately jumped on the band wagon and bought sound systems.

The Hackberry Ramblers are still playing music and feel a sense of pride and accomplishment in having been part of the evolution of amplification of string music in dance halls.

Bon Ton Café

Submitted by the Bon Ton Café

Bon Ton Café is famous for its Southern Louisiana Bayou cooking known as "Cajun." The owners (the Pierce family) are from Bayou Laforche in southeast Louisiana and have been operating the café since 1953. Their claim to fame is their wonderful bread pudding and their crawfish cooked in the New Orleans tradition.

Bread Pudding

Submitted by Wayne Pierce, Bon Ton Café

6 ounces	stale French bread with crust
2 cups	milk
2	eggs
1 cup	sugar
1 stick	margarine, melted
4 Tablespoons	vanilla
¼ cup	raisins
1½ Tablespoons	butter or margarine, melted

Whiskey sauce:

1 cup	sugar
1	egg
1 stick	butter, melted
6 ounces	whiskey

To make the pudding, break the bread into pieces and place in large bowl. Add the milk until the bread absorbs it. Add eggs, sugar, margarine, vanilla, and raisins, and stir well. Coat the bottom of the baking pan with additional margarine. Select a pan that will allow the pudding to be 1½ inches in thickness (pan size should be approximately 4 inches × 6 inches × 3 inches deep). Pour the bread mixture into the pan. Bake at 350° approximately 45 minutes or until the pudding is firm and light golden brown. Let the pudding cool. Cut the pudding into individual portions, put each in separate dessert dish.

To make the whiskey sauce, cream or mix the sugar and egg. Add the butter, and stir until the sugar is dissolved. A small amount of water (1½ ounces) may be needed to aid in dissolving the sugar. Stir in the whiskey.

When ready to serve, pour sauce over pudding in individual dessert dish and heat under broiler. **Serves:** 6

Mardi Gras

Courtesy of Riverwalk

There are two "local" terms for New Orleans' famous pre-Easter celebration. The first is Mardi Gras, French for Fat Tuesday, because it always falls on the Tuesday before Ash Wednesday, the first day of Lent. (The term refers to the old custom of leading a fattened ox through the streets of a Catholic village. The ox was the final meat meal before Lent.) The second term is the word Carnival, which comes from the Latin roots "carne" and "valle" meaning farewell to flesh. The expressions are significant since they point up the importance of the holiday in both religious and secular terms.

To trace the beginning of New Orleans carnival, we must go back 150 years. In the mid-1830's, the Creoles decided to emulate the carnivals which have prevailed for centuries in some areas of Europe. The motto was "Have a jolly good time before you start strict fast and abstinence." The first New Orleans celebrations were held in an edifice (still standing) on Orleans Street between Royal and Bourbon Streets, but the fun spilled out of the building. The revelry continued in marching and dancing in the streets of the French Quarter. Male celebrants (for fear of creating a social scandal) wore masks so that they could not be identified.

Shortly after the birth of Mardi Gras, rowdyism began to mar the celebration. Though nothing more than minor injuries resulted from flying sacks of flour and the like, the custom was suspended for a few years and was resumed shortly before the Civil War.

Since then, New Orleans Mardi Gras has become one of the best loved and most elaborate carnivals in the world. There are musicians, dancers, and parades with elaborate floats, carrying masked revelers who toss plastic beads and aluminum dubloons to crowds lining the streets. Societies called krewes organize and pay for parades, private parties and other festivities. From the Twelfth Night or Epiphany (January 6), the beginning of the Carnival Season, to the Fat Tuesday Celebration commemorating the beginning of Lent, New Orleanians concentrate on partying—which they do so well.

Marty Grog

Submitted by Joe Pando, New Orleans
Original Daiquiris, Riverwalk

A deliciously refreshing frozen drink that is both fruity and pungent.

1⅓ ounces	light rum
1⅓ ounces	dark rum
1⅓ ounces	grapefruit juice
1 ounce	orange juice
1 ounce	pineapple juice
2 8-ounce cups	filled with crushed ice

Place all ingredients in blender and blend on medium speed for about 30 seconds, or until a slushy, frozen texture is achieved. For a stronger drink, substitute 151 proof for the dark rum. **Hint:** If using ice cubes instead of crushed ice, use less ice and blend on highest speed. If using shaved ice, use more ice and blend at slower speed. **Yield:** 2 8 ounce servings

Jacques Cocktail of Roquefort

Submitted by Mary Michael

1 pound	roquefort cheese
2 sticks	unsalted butter
5 Tablespoons	cognac

Beat roquefort in food processor until smooth. Add butter. Place in bowl over hot water and whisk in cognac. Serve as a spread with water crackers or sliced french bread. The spread will keep in refrigerator 2 months.

Shrimp on Cracker

Submitted by Mercedes Andrus

The best canapé of all, according to all guests.

1 pound	medium cheddar
1 pint	mayonnaise
	salt and red pepper
	to taste
1 pound	shrimp
1 box	Ritz® crackers
	hamburger-
	dill sliced pickles

Grate cheese very fine, add mayonnaise, salt and pepper. Boil shrimp in highly seasoned water for 5 minutes, peel, cool, and marinate in cheese and mayonnaise sauce for 2 or 3 hours. To serve, place pickle on Ritz cracker, top with shrimp and cover with cheese sauce. Bake in 350° oven until bubbly, about 3 minutes. **Serves: 8:**

"Mardi Gras"
Blanquette De Veau

Submitted by Mrs. Oliver A. Billion Sr., Queen of Rex, 1915

2 pounds	breast of veal
1	onion, quartered
1 teaspoon	salt and
	pepper to taste
1	carrot
	bay leaf and
	sprig of parsley or
	bouquet garni
2 Tablespoons	butter
1 Tablespoon	flour
2	egg yolks
1 cup	cream

Cut veal into cubes, pour boiling, salted water over it, and let soak for twenty minutes. Drain veal and put in a pan; cover with water. Add onion, salt, pepper, carrot (sliced in quarters), bay leaf and sprig of parsley. Bring to a boil and simmer slowly for about one hour, or until veal is tender. When meat is done, make a white sauce with butter, flour and meat stock. Cook for twenty minutes and add egg yolks mixed with cream. Pour over meat and serve in casserole. **Variation:** This may be served with small, white onions. Put onions, cooked until tender, in casserole with veal and pour sauce over all. Mushrooms, cooked separately, may be used in the same way with the veal. **Serves:** 4-6

Croquignolles, Aunt Rose's Mardi Gras Doughnuts

Submitted by Alcée-Hymel Family

Maskers used to come by the house and people would give them croquignolles with coffee.

2 cups	flour
2 Tablespoons	sugar
2 teaspoons	baking powder
½ cup	milk
2	eggs
	pinch of salt
1 teaspoon	pure vanilla extract
	oil for deep frying
	powdered sugar

Mix flour, sugar and baking powder together. Make a well in the middle and add the milk, eggs, a pinch of salt and the vanilla. Beat these together and gradually work in the flour. Roll out on a floured board to about ¼ inch, or a little thinner if preferred.

Cut the dough into 2 × 4-inch strips and simply make 3 or 4 slits in the center. Fry in deep oil until golden brown. Sprinkle with powdered sugar. **Hint:** These will be firmer than doughnuts.

Yield: approximately 18-20

Hot Spiced Holiday Grog

Submitted by Joanne Amorte, Oak Alley Plantation

1 gallon	dry white wine
1 cup	sugar
¼ cup	lemon juice
6	cinnamon sticks
½ gallon	apple juice or cider
½ cup	water
24	whole cloves
	orange slices, whole cloves and cinnamon sticks for garnish

Mix all ingredients in large saucepan. Simmer for 20-30 minutes. Serve steaming hot in decorative ceramic or silver punch bowl. Garnish with fresh orange slices and whole cloves. Pour into holiday coffee mugs with a cinnamon stick in each.
Yield: 5 quarts

King Cake

Submitted by Carol H. Massarini

Officially, the Carnival season can be short or long, depending on when Lent and Easter fall on the given year's calendar. But the start of the Mardi Gras season is always Twelfth Night (the twelfth day after Christmas), which commemorates the visit of the Three Wise Men to Bethlehem. Among the Spanish, Twelfth Night, rather than Christmas, is the day when gifts are presented. Among the French, it is Petit Noel, or Little Christmas, on January 6th, when balls are held.

Traditionally, the opening celebrations took place in private homes and culminated in the eating of the Gateau du Roi, or King's Cake, made of brioche batter. Hidden away somewhere in the cakes was either a small bisque or china doll, or a bean, usually a red bean and sometimes covered in silver or gold leaf. The person who chose the piece of cake with the bean or doll became the king or queen of the ball. He or she was then responsible for holding the next ball in the next week. These weekend balls continued until Mardi Gras itself. (Among the wealthy, actual gold and diamond jewelry is sometimes substituted for the bean or doll.)

To make the cake, use a recipe for true butter and yeast brioche, formed into a great ring on a baking sheet. After baking, sprinkle the cake with alternating bands of sugar dyed purple, yellow and green, the Carnival colors. Don't forget to bake in a bean or doll but, for the traditional, avoid plastic dolls.

New Orleans King Cake

Submitted by Carol H. Massarini

2 Tablespoons	sugar
2 envelopes	of dry active yeast
7/8 cup	warm water
1 stick	butter
7/8 cup	evaporated milk
1/2 cup	sugar
2 teaspoons	salt
4	eggs
5 cups	flour
1/2 box	brown sugar
1 cup	granulated sugar
2 Tablespoons	cinnamon
1 stick	butter, melted
1 cup	confectioners sugar
2 Tablespoons	milk
1/4 cup	sugar, tinted green
1/4 cup	sugar, tinted yellow
1/4 cup	sugar, tinted purple

Combine sugar, yeast and water in bowl. Let stand until foaming. Place butter, milk, sugar, and salt in small pot and melt slowly.

Beat eggs into foaming yeast, and add milk mixture when it is lukewarm.

Add flour, a little at a time. Knead for 5-10 minutes. Grease a bowl with margarine, place dough in bowl, turn dough over in bowl and then cover bowl with wet cloth. Let rise until double, about 1 or 2 hours, in a warm place. While dough is rising, mix sugars and cinnamon.

Punch dough down when doubled. Roll out to about 18″ × 36″. Brush with melted butter and sprinkle with sugar mixture.

Cut into three strips, rolling each like a jelly roll, then braid. Cover with a wet cloth and let rise until double again. Place a little doll in one of the rolls, after braiding.

Bake at 350° for 20 to 30 minutes. When cooled, spread top with glaze made of confectioners sugar and milk. Sprinkle with tinted sugars that have been mixed together. You may need to make the icing 3 times to cover cake. **Serves:** approximately 30

Festival Garlic Bread

Submitted by Al Copeland, Copeland's of New Orleans

1 loaf	French bread
1 stick	unsalted butter or margarine, softened
2	garlic cloves, minced or pressed
½ teaspoon	cayenne pepper
½ cup	sharp Cheddar cheese, grated
½ cup	Monterey Jack cheese, grated

Cut French bread into 1-inch slices. Mash softened butter, garlic and cayenne until easy to spread. Coat each slice of French bread with butter mixture. Mix grated cheeses together and sprinkle over bread. Lay bread flat on cookie sheet, cheese side up. Place in 450° oven for 10-12 minutes, until brown and bubbly. **Yield:** 1 loaf

Offerings of Food: The Custom of St. Joseph Altars

Courtesy of Riverwalk

St. Joseph's Day, March 19th, has become an important holiday for Roman Catholics in New Orleans, especially for those of Italian descent. Even though St. Joseph's falls during Lent, the period of fasting and abstinence before Easter, dancing and feasting are allowed on this festival day.

The most colorful ritual of St. Joseph's Day is the practice of setting up "St. Joseph's Day altars." Several hundred years ago, in days of political persecution, a group of Italians were put on a ship and cast adrift without food. Day and night they prayed to St. Joseph (the protector of the holy family) to save them. When they reached landfall in Sicily, they prepared a feast for the hungry in the saint's honor. Most of the Italian immigrants to New Orleans were from Sicily, and they brought this custom with them.

Home altars are decorated with paper flowers, lace cloths, statues of saints and candles. They are heaped high with good things to eat, symbolizing the Lord's bounty, including Sicilian breads, cheeses and desserts; baked seafood; stuffed artichokes, eggplants and bell peppers; and avocados (called alligator pears locally). The altar is blessed by a priest, and a brief ritual is staged, with children impersonating Jesus, Mary and Joseph. Visitors partake freely. After having fallen into disuse, the custom recently has gone through a revival, with the largest altar being placed in the Piazza d'Italia on Poydras Street near Riverwalk.

St. Joseph's Day Fig Cookies

Submitted by Virginia Fontana

Virginia Fontana bakes these cookies for the St. Joseph's Day altar and they have been enjoyed by all who come. Though she is in her eighties, she is still there every year with her cookies.

Dough:

4 large or 5 medium	eggs
3 cups	white granulated sugar
3 cups	Crisco® or 1.3 ounces on scale
3 Tablespoons	vanilla
5 pounds	plain flour
3 Tablespoons	baking powder
1 teaspoon	salt
⅔ quart	fresh milk (approximately)

In large bowl, work eggs and sugar together by hand. Add shortening, working until smooth, then vanilla.

Sift together flour and baking powder, add salt. Then add these dry ingredients to the egg mixture using a creaming motion, about ¼ of the amount at a time, alternating with milk until all flour is used. When all the flour is mixed well and the proper amount of milk is used the dough will form a large ball in the center of bowl, leaving the sides of the bowl clean. (It sometimes takes less than ⅔ quart of milk.) This dough is better if made ahead of time and chilled.

Filling:

3 packages (1 pound each)	**dried figs (remove stems)**
½ pound	**dates (pits removed)**
2 pounds	**mixed glazed fruits**
1 box (15 ounces)	**dried raisins**
8 ounces	**glazed red and green pineapple**
8 ounces	**glazed red and green cherries**
2 cups	**nuts (pecans, almonds, walnuts)**
	juice and grated rind of 2 naval oranges
1 cup	**sugar**
1 teaspoon	**ground cinnamon**
¾ teaspoon	**ground cloves**
¾ teaspoon	**ground allspice**
1 quart	**apple juice**
1 cup	**rum (optional)**

Quarter dried figs, cut dates in half. Mix dried figs, glazed fruits, dates, raisins, glazed pineapples, cherries and nuts, grated orange rind and juice, and grind together. Dissolve sugar, ground cinnamon, ground cloves and ground allspice in apple juice. Place fruit mixture in pot with apple juice and spices and heat until warm and blended together well. Cool mixture.

Roll piece of dough flat, cut into 3-inch strips and put filling down the middle of this strip about the thickness of your finger. Fold one edge of the dough over the filling, then the other side over the first side, sealing fruit mix on the inside. Turn folded side to bottom and cut strip in pieces about 1½ to 2 inches long. Place on cookie sheet or pans ¾-inch apart. Bake in 350° oven for 15-20 minutes until light brown. Cool.

Icing:

1 box	powdered sugar
1 stick	butter, melted
2 teaspoons	vanilla
	evaporated milk for
	desired thickness
	few drops of lemon
	juice for drying

Mix together powdered sugar, melted butter and vanilla. Add evaporated milk for desired thickness. Divide icing into 4 or 5 little bowls using a few drops of lemon juice in each to cause icing to dry quickly. Use food coloring to color each bowl differently and ice baked cookies with small brush. Then decorate top with different colored cake decorations. **Yield:** dozens and dozens

Agnolotti Pasta (Ravioli)

Submitted by Goffredo Fraccaro, La Riviera Restaurant

4 cups	all purpose flour
2	eggs
1 pinch	salt
1 cup	water

Put the flour on a large pastry board. Make a well in the middle and add the eggs, water and salt. Work the eggs and water into the flour, then knead to a smooth elastic dough for about 10 minutes.

Roll the dough out as thinly as possible in two sheets. On one sheet arrange teaspoons of the stuffing (see instructions for stuffing, following) in little heaps at regular intervals, 1½ inch apart.

Cover with the second sheet of dough and press with the finger around the heaps of stuffing. Cut the Agnolotti square with a pastry wheel and make quite sure the edges are firmly sealed.

Sprinkle lightly with flour and let them rest for 30 minutes, turning them after 15 minutes.

Bring a large pan of salt water to boil, and the Agnolotti and cook for 12 minutes. Lift out with a perforated spoon and transfer to a heated serving dish.

Add sauce (see instructions for sauce, following) and top with additional parmesan cheese. **Serves:** 6

Agnolotti Alla Fraccaro
(Crabmeat Sauce)

Submitted by Goffredo Fraccaro, La Riviera Restaurant

Bechamel Thick Sauce:

½ cup	milk
1 Tablespoon	butter
1 Tablespoon	flour
¼ teaspoon	salt
	pinch of white and red pepper
1	egg yolk

Cook together, then let cool.

Stuffing:

½ cup	chopped green onion
1 Tablespoon	butter
1	egg white
2 Tablespoons	parsley
1 pound	crabmeat
4 Tablespoons	cracker crumbs

Sauté green onion in butter. Add remaining ingredients to pan. Mix stuffing together with Bechamel Thick Sauce.

Sauce:

1 cup	whipping cream (reduce by ½)
½ stick	butter
	salt, red and white pepper to taste

Cook all ingredients until slight boil.

Cauliflower Cake

Submitted by the Bergeron Family

1 medium	cauliflower
1	egg
	Italian bread crumbs
	Parmesan cheese
8 Tablespoons	olive oil, approximately
	salt and pepper to taste

Boil cauliflower until tender. Remove and strain off water. Place in bowl and mash. Add egg, and enough Italian crumbs and Parmesan cheese to make desired consistency and mix together. Put about 4 tablespoons of olive oil in frying pan and heat. Add mixture and press flat. Cook on medium until brown, then flip over in plate. Wash frying pan and fry cauliflower on other side. **Serves:** 4 as a side dish

The Good Luck Bean

Submitted by Virginia Fontana

The Lucky Bean—The most popular and best known custom of the St. Joseph Altar is the "fava" or lucky bean. Legend has it that during one of the famines in Sicily, some farmers discovered that the fava bean would grow well even in poor soil. Hence it became a life saving crop and was referred to as the lucky bean. Fava beans are given away on the feast day and are said to bring good luck to those who carry them all year.

Louisiana Fig Bread

Submitted by Betty Comeaux

1½ cups	unbleached white flour
⅔ cup	sugar
1½ teaspoons	baking powder
½ teaspoon	salt
2	eggs
½ cup	milk
⅓ cup	oil
1 teaspoon	vanilla
⅓ cup	brown sugar
½ teaspoon	cinnamon
2 Tablespoons	butter
10	fig bar cookies, crumbled

Combine flour, sugar, baking powder and salt and set aside. Combine eggs, milk, oil and vanilla. Stir this mixture into flour mixture. Pour ½ of batter into greased/floured 8½ × 4½ × 2½-inch loaf pan. Combine brown sugar, cinnamon and cut in butter. Add crumbled fig bar cookies to this mixture. Add ½ of fig bar/sugar mixture to batter in pan. Pour rest of batter on top, then rest of fig bar/sugar mixture. Swirl with a knife. Bake at 350° for about 1 hour. **Yield:** 1 fig bread

Pasta With Shrimp Sauce

Submitted by Nicole Ferrier, Ralph & Kacoo's Restaurants

⅓ cup	olive oil
½ cup	garlic, chopped
1 cup	green pepper, chopped
1 cup	onion, chopped
3 cups	fresh tomatoes, chopped
1 Tablespoon	basil
1 Tablespoon	oregano
	salt, red pepper flakes and ground black pepper to taste
½ cup	butter
1 pound (36-42)	raw shrimp, peeled
1 cup	parsley, chopped
1 pound	spaghetti
	parmesan cheese

Heat olive oil. Sauté garlic, green pepper and onion until soft. Add tomatoes, basil, oregano, salt, red pepper, and black pepper. Cover and cook for ½ hour. Add butter, peeled shrimp and parsley. Simmer until shrimp are cooked. Cook spaghetti in separate pot. Mix sauce with spaghetti and serve with parmesan cheese on the side. **Serves:** 6-8

Shrimp Mosca
(Barbecued Shrimp)

Submitted by Chiqui Collier, Cookery N'Orleans Style Restaurant

5 pounds	**large shrimp (shells on heads add plenty of flavor but headless do just as well)**

per batch:

¼ inch	**deep strong olive oil**
1 Tablespoon	**rosemary**
1 teaspoon	**crushed red pepper flakes**
1 teaspoon	**black pepper, coarsely ground**
1 Tablespoon	**dried minced garlic**
½ cup	**sauterne wine**

In a heavy skillet heat olive oil ¼-inch deep in pan. Add a double layer of shrimp and all the dried seasonings. Fry on high about 5 minutes. Add the wine and cover. Lower heat and cook 10 minutes. Repeat 2 times (5 pounds of shrimp should yield about 3 batches). Prepare shrimp about 1 hour before serving. Toss well while marinating. Reheat to serve. Pass plenty of French bread and napkins. Serve in a deep soup bowl and top with sauce. The sauce serves as a dip for the French bread.
Serves: 10-12

Cities of the Dead

Submitted by Winnie B. Traina (excerpts from "A Cemetery in a Church" by R. A. McGuire) St. Louis Cemetery Number One

Situated in the four hundred block of Basin Street, facing east and occupying a square block, is the nation's oldest cemetery. It is still in use and is known as St. Louis Number One.

Although it bares the same name as the St. Louis Cathedral it was not named after the church, but after Louis XIV of France. Within its brick walls one finds the alleys between the tombs crooked and tortuous, making the exit for strangers hard to locate. Many of the tombs are the property of bygone settlers. Should the visitor take the time, he or she would note on many a crumbling tomb, the party interred therein had a vital part in the early history of the city. One of the most frequent inscriptions found: "Mort sur le champ d'honneur," or "Victime d l'honneur." This is French meaning: "Here lies one who fell in a duel."

To most tourists, New Orleans' method of interring her dead is a horrible way of "putting away loved ones." However, if today's visitor could have seen the city a hundred or more years ago he or she would readily understand why. Prior to the establishment of a modern drainage system, water was found at from one to two feet below the surface of the ground. Hence the orthodox method of a grave six feet beneath the surface of the ground was out of the question, unless one had no objection of placing a body in a grave filled with water.

The tombs, or vaults as some choose to call them, contain but one body at a time. Nevertheless many bodies have been entombed in the same compartment. This is due to a state law, in part reading: A tomb, or vault must remain sealed for a year and a day after a burial therein. After that time has expired the vault may be opened and used again.

In preparing a vault or tomb for use, the sexton removes the bricks that are used to seal the opening. Next, he removes the casket or what remains of it.

The bones are placed in the rear of the vault thereby making room for another body to be placed therein. With few exceptions this rule still prevails. (The city, however, has one cemetery where this rule does not prevail. For here, once a body has been interred the vault is never opened.)

In the last few years the drainage system has been greatly extended and it is now possible to bury directly into the ground, and this mode of burial is becoming more and more popular. (This, however, is not true of cremating. It seems the native has a deep rooted horror of cremation.)

A Nickel Here, a Nickel There

Submitted by George Reinecke

In the days before the Civil War, a Marylander named John McDonogh rose to importance in New Orleans as a wealthy man of business. He lived on the west bank of the Mississippi in what is today called McDonoghville, between Algiers and Gretna proper. Each day he would come to do business in New Orleans. But he did not come in by the "Picayune Ferry" which would have dropped him at the foot of Canal Street and cost one silver half-dime. Instead, he had one of his servants row him across in a skiff he maintained for this purpose. McDonogh was known as a miser of the worst sort. Today, however, he is remembered as the donor of the New Orleans' City Park and the founder of an education fund which provided for the construction of more than forty public schools over the decades, eighteen of which still bear his name. Opposite Old City Hall, now called Gallier Hall, there is a bust of McDonogh on a marble pedestal, and below, a small boy and girl in bronze reach up to offer flowers to their benefactor. Each year, children from the public schools gather at the monument and lay flowers at the foot of the statue, and sing, "He gave his funds to educate. . ." to the tune of "Maryland, My Maryland." The nickels saved from the Canal Street Ferry added up!

Maryland Style Louisiana Crab Soup

Submitted by Joann Myles

1	ham bone
2	bay leaves
1	whole onion, sliced pieces of ham from the bone
3 stalks	celery, diced
3	carrots, sliced
½ cup	macaroni
3	ears corn, cut into bite-size pieces
½ cup	lima beans
½ head	cabbage, chopped
1 can (1 pound)	tomatoes
1 pound	crabmeat
2 heavy Tablespoons	Zatarain's® crab boil (in Maryland use "Old Bay®")
	pepper to taste
2 teaspoons	Worcestershire sauce
1 heavy teaspoon	prepared mustard
2 Tablespoons	vinegar
2 small	boiled crabs if desired (if in Maryland steam the crabs)

Put ham bone in dutch oven and fill half way with water. Add bay leaves and onion. Cook 1 hour and strain. To this stock add ham bits, celery, carrots, macaroni, corn, lima beans, cabbage, tomatoes and crabmeat. In a separate bowl, mix Zatarain's crab boil, pepper to taste, Worcestershire sauce, mustard and vinegar. Stir up and add to pot. If desired, add 2 small crabs at this point. Cook for 2½ hours. **Note:** Marylanders do things differently than New Orleanians. Therefore, we have included special instructions for them! **Serves:** 6-8

Chapter II
Tall Tales

New Orleans is rich in wonderful folklore. The following chapter has some legends that we call "Tall Tales" and quite a few unbelievable recipes—believe it or not!

Magnolia Plantation

Submitted by Sylvia Stanton

The Magnolia Plantation has a strange history. It was originally owned by John Landon, Jr. in 1889 and was purchased by Robert and Sylvia Stanton in 1974. They had six children and the house was always busy. Sylvia had decorated it in light airy colors and she always felt loved and protected in it. One night, after returning home from a party, the Stantons heard running and laughter as they approached the house. They thought, "It's late and we've caught the children running to jump into bed before we come in." But when they entered the front door they remembered that every child was someplace else (date or slumber party, depending on age). They looked all over and could find nothing.

The next event occurred when their ten year old walked downstairs to get something from the refrigerator. She started to go back upstairs and looked up to see a fat gentleman in a white suit looking down at her from the top step. She said he looked like Colonel Sanders. Twice after that, she saw him and once she saw a thin young man dressed in black leaning over the foot of her bed just looking down at her while she slept.

Mrs. Stanton says, "A few years after that our son had a friend from college spending a few weeks with us while he found a job. One morning at 5 a.m., we heard him screaming and when we checked on him, he said it was only a bad dream. Later he admitted that during the night he had seen a pale blonde haired girl looking at him from the foot of the bed and that she had had a green glow around her face. I told him of the other happenings and that afternoon he left."

"A few years later when our daughter was engaged, she told her boyfriend about 'Colonel San-

75

ders' and he teased her about it. One night when the house was empty except for them, they both heard footsteps upstairs. He looked under beds and closets but no one was there. My daughter still hates the house, but I love it. It means no harm. I feel strange sometimes but that is all. I know if there are 'guests' they seem to like us and are sociable.

Stanton Manor is now open to the public for parties, weddings and business Seminars

Chicken Magnolia

Submitted by Chef Sylvia Stanton, Magnolia Plantation

The following recipe is the favorite of owners Robert and Sylvia Stanton.

4 breasts	**of chicken**
1	**eggplant**
½ cup	**Progresso Italian Seasoned Crumbs®**
½ cup	**cooked, peeled shrimp (cut in half)**
	white chicken sauce
	parsley for garnish

Debone the breasts but be careful not to loosen skin. Wrap whole eggplant in Saran Wrap®, place in bowl and microwave for 8 minutes. Take out to cool and when cool, unwrap and cut into quarters. The seeds can be easily removed now. Peel back purple skin. Discard skin and seeds. Mash pulp with a fork and mix in bread crumbs and shrimp. Form into 4 balls and lay breasts out flat with skin side down. Flatten a bit more with your hand and add 1 eggplant ball and fold meat around ball, turning it over so skin side shows. Shape it to look like a neat triangle. Put in a pan, brush with oil and lightly sprinkle with salt and pepper. Cook at 325° for 30 minutes until done. Breast will be nicely browned. Spoon a creamy white chicken sauce over the top of each breast and garnish with a sprig of parsley. Delicious and pretty for a special occasion.
Serves: 4

The Madstone of Vacherie

Submitted by Joanne Amorte, Oak Alley Plantation

This story begins one day almost 200 years ago when a Chickasaw Indian came to the Vacherie area to trade with the frugal and hard working Germans. During his stay he became gravely ill, and was sheltered and nursed back to health by a kindly German settler named Josef Webre. Shortly before the convalescent left his benefactor's care, one of the ladies of the Webre household went to her garden to cut a cabbage for dinner. Instead of the succulent vegetable she already imagined stewing in the soup pot, what she got for her culinary efforts was a nasty bite from a rattlesnake! Seeing the confusion and terror surrounding the plight of the poor lady, the Indian ran to his pirogue and returned with a small, flat, blackish-brown stone which he applied to the wound and, to the amazement of all, the suffering victim recovered. A strong tie of friendship between the Chickasaw and Herr Webre was born of these circumstances and the Indian remained with the Webres a year. When he left to return to his people, as a token of gratitude, he gave the miraculous stone to Josef Webre. The stone has remained in the custody of the Gravois-Webre family to this day. Its secure resting place is in a tin can bearing the remarkably apt label "Indian Ointment!"

Countless stories have surrounded the "Mad Stone" of Vacherie in the years since its appearance on the scene. Its benefits are, apparently, limited to cures for bites by venomous snakes and rabid animals as well as various types of infection from poisonous plants. All of the accounts are of miraculous cures, none of failures! The stone is thought to draw out venom. When placed on an infected wound, the stone clings to it as if by magnetic force, and users say that the pain disappears rapidly. It will not adhere to a fresh cut. . .only where there is poison. The patient may move about freely without dislodging the stone, which will not loosen its hold until all traces of infection are withdrawn. After use, the stone is carefully washed in cold water, at which time yet another interesting reaction can be observed. . .the water bubbles, as if boiling, when the stone is immersed! When all activity ceases the stone is removed and carefully wrapped in cotton before being returned to its metal container.

Many offers have been made to buy the stone, but it is definitely not for sale! It has been out of the household on only one occasion when its owner took it to New Orleans for examination in an effort to determine possible medical reasons for its strange powers. Doctors and scientists photographed it from every angle and examined it under high-powered microscopes, but it never showed any qualities other than those of an ordinary stone. The learned men were baffled!

What is it? Faith? Coincidence? Magic? No one knows! In almost two centuries there has not been one logical explanation for this phenomenon. The fact is that the "Mad Stone" of Vacherie exists, and it works today just as it always had—"Believe It Or Not!"

Oak Alley Restaurant's Crab Dip

Submitted by Joanne Amorte, Oak Alley Plantation

6 ounces	frozen chopped broccoli
½ pound	butter
¾ cup	chopped onion
½ cup	chopped celery
1½ teaspoons	basil
4 ounces	mushrooms, chopped
½ cup	chopped artichoke hearts
1 teaspoon	garlic, chopped
⅛ cup	lemon juice
1 teaspoon	Pickapeppa®
2 Tablespoons	piquant sauce
1½ teaspoons	Italian seasoning
2½ cans	cream of mushroom soup (approximately 26 ounces)
1½ teaspoons	Tony's Seasoning® (Tony Chachere)
½ cup	chablis
½ pound	cream cheese
¼ cup	Half & Half®
⅛ cup	shredded mixed cheese
1 pound	crabmeat
¼ teaspoon	ground nutmeg

Boil broccoli in salted water and drain well. Melt butter in large saucepan. Sauté onions, celery, basil, mushrooms, artichoke hearts, and garlic until onions are clear. Add cooked broccoli, lemon juice, Pickapeppa, piquant sauce, Italian seasoning, mushroom soup and Tony's seasoning and sauté for 20 minutes. Stir in wine and cook on low flame for 5 minutes. Process cream cheese with Half & Half and add to dip. Cook until melted. Add shredded mixed cheese and simmer until melted. Stir in crab-meat and nutmeg and cook on low flame about 15 minutes.

Serve hot in a chafing dish with corn chips and crackers. **Yields:** 2½ quarts

Clean Sweep-Up

Submitted by Brooke Taylor

Many years ago there was a pirate named Phillipe. When he wasn't on ship, he boarded at the Widow Hebert's home in the French Quarter. Phillipe loved Mardi Gras parades but he hated the trash and debris left over from the parades. It became an obsession with Phillipe and his crews to clean up after Mardi Gras while the rest of the city slept. To this day, long after Phillipe's death, we wonder how the city gets cleaned up so quickly after Fat Tuesday. There are those who still hear pirates chanting late on Mardi Gras night and when we awaken to a clean city on Ash Wednesday, we wonder!

Eggs Riverbend

Submitted by Louise Glickman

Riverbend is a favorite breakfast and brunch stop for anyone who gets up early (Regulars arrive daily with the staff at 6:30 a.m., catch up on local news with friends, read their papers and sip the good black coffee knowing that the biscuits will be out at 7:15.) Others know that breakfast is served throughout the day at the Riverbend, and they often arrive late at night for a delicious Riverbend omelet or other brunch specialty. Looking for a slant on the traditional "twins", Eggs Benedict and Eggs Sardou, the Riverbend developed Eggs Riverbend for those who can't seem to make up their minds! It is a customer favorite.

1-2	English muffins open, buttered and toasted
2-4 slices	Canadian bacon
4-6 cups	grated mozzarella cheese
2-4	poached eggs
3-4 cups	Hollandaise sauce

Spinach Mixture:

3 pounds	spinach
1 pound	mushrooms, sliced
1 large	white onion, chopped
1 Tablespoon	garlic powder
1 Tablespoon	white pepper
2 Tablespoons	chicken base

Spinach mixture: cook all ingredients together, uncovered for about ½ hour until soft and blended. To serve: top English muffin with one piece Canadian bacon, mozzarella cheese, spinach mixture, poached egg and Hollandaise sauce. Bon Appetit!
Serves: 1-2

Fiddler's Folk Tale

Submitted by Bill Kirkpatrick, of the Louisiana Hayride
(a travelling group of fiddlers)

These two old hound dogs named Blue and Bell were laying down on the porch taking it easy. Along came some kids and they cranked up the old "Victrolar." They put one of those old jazz records on and cranked it up and let it go. They went to dancing, shaking and looking like a snake wiggling. They were really getting with it.

Old Blue looked at old Bell (scratching a few fleas) and said to her, "Bell, if me and you acted like them der kids, our master would worm us wouldn't he?"

"Lazy" Brunch Eggs

Submitted by Mary Michael

8 slices	bread
¾ cup	sharp cheddar cheese
1½ cups	ham or polish sausage
½ cup	canned mushrooms
2 Tablespoons	green pepper
1 Tablespoon	pimento
3 cups	milk
4	eggs
1 teaspoon	dry mustard

Tear bread and place in buttered baking dish, add cubed cheese, diced ham (if using sausage, slice and lightly sauté), mushrooms, chopped green pepper and pimento. Mix milk, slightly beaten egg and dry mustard. Pour over ingredients in dish and bake at 350° for 40 minutes or until brown. Serve immediately. **Hint:** may be made the day before and baked before serving. **Serves:** 6

Napoleon Bonaparte House

Submitted by the Napoleon House Bar & Café

Napoleon Bonaparte House is located at the corner of St. Louis and Chartres Streets, in the heart of the French Quarter of New Orleans. The Napoleon House Bar, favored by artists and writers, is famous for its fine collection of classical records, played at the request of patrons. The building was built as a refuge for Napoleon Bonaparte, as part of a plan to rescue him from exile at St. Helena and bring him to New Orleans. Napoleon died before this plan was fulfilled and although he never set foot on Louisiana soil, the legend of Napoleon Bonaparte looms as large as the state itself.

The Napoleon House Muffaletta

Submitted by Sal Impastato, Napoleon House Bar & Café

4 slices	ham
5 slices	genoa salami
4 slices	pastrami
	Italian olive salad, spread evenly
3 slices	provalone cheese
2 slices	swiss cheese
1	muffaletta bun

Layer the above ingredients on a muffaletta bun. Cut into 4 pieces and warm in a microwave oven or wrapped in foil in a conventional oven. **Hint:** The bread is a big factor in the taste of this sandwich. The bread used by the Napoleon House Bar and Café comes from an Italian Bakery that has been baking these buns since the turn of the century. **Serves: 2**

The Axeman's Jazz

In 1919 a series of brutal axe murders took place in New Orleans. Someone took out a classified ad announcing the imminent reappearance of the axeman in the Crescent City, and that every household where a jazz band was playing would be spared. On the appointed date an astonishing number of parties were given as Orleanians awaited the dreaded murderer. A piece of music was published entitled "The Axeman's Jazz" which enjoyed short, sensational popularity. Speculation is that the advertisement was the semi-practical joke of an out of work jazz musician.

"Musician's" Mushrooms Marinade

Submitted by Mrs. William G. Zetzmann

1 pound	medium mushrooms
2 Tablespoons	butter
2 Tablespoons	water
2 Tablespoons	minced celery
½ cup	vinegar
½ teaspoon	freshly ground black pepper
1 Tablespoon	minced parsley
1 clove	garlic
1	lemon
	juice of 1 lemon
½ cup	olive oil
1	bay leaf
1 pinch	oregano
	parsley for garnish

Simmer mushrooms in butter and water for 5 minutes. Combine in bowl with the remaining ingredients that have been simmered together for five minutes. Cool and place in refrigerator to absorb the flavor of marinade. Serve on toast rounds. Sprinkle lightly with parsley.

Man Plant (People Potatoes)

Courtesy of Riverwalk

The first settlers in New Orleans encountered many strange foods not found in Europe, like the man plant. It was a wild potato resembling the Irish potato, yet bigger than the largest yam. It had the shape and face of a human being with the features of the face clearly marked; a neck, shoulders, and a well defined body. Some had male features and others female features. They huddled together as if in a settlement and they trembled when touched and even seemed to move away as if to protect themselves. It was truly a hostile and strange land; even the plants fought back!

Creamy Potato Salad

Submitted by Mayor and Mrs. Sidney J. Barthelemy

3 large	Irish potatoes
½ medium	onion, chopped
¼ cup	fresh parsley, chopped
3	boiled eggs, diced
½ cup	mayonnaise
1 teaspoon	vinegar
	salt and pepper to taste

Boil potatoes until tender when pricked with a fork. Place onion and parsley in bowl. Peel and cut hot potatoes into chunks. Mash hot potatoes over onions and parsley. Add eggs and mix. Add other ingredients and mix well. Serve hot or cold.
Serves: 6

Potato Balls

Submitted by Paul Constantin, Constantin's Restaurant

These potato balls were created by my wife Patti, (co-owner of Constantin's). This particular recipe can be somewhat temperamental because of the water content in the potatoes. These poor potato balls have been called many an ungracious name by cooks in our kitchen, who didn't know how to remedy a disintegrating ball during the middle of a busy dinner!

5	baking potatoes
2-3	whole eggs (raw)
3 ounces	swiss cheese, chopped
½ bunch	green onions
	sprinkle of finely grated parmesan cheese
	salt and pepper (red and black) to taste

Boil potatoes until slightly undercooked. Let them drain and cool. Add all of the ingredients plus 2 of the 3 raw eggs (beaten). Mash the potatoes until just small pieces of potato remain. (Do not use mixer.) Roll a test ball 1½ inches in diameter. Test it by dipping in fryer 350°. If the ball doesn't stay together, add the final egg to help bind it.

Hint: If for some reason the recipe doesn't work, the potatoes have too much water in them. Then you must resort to a slight coating of bread crumbs.
Serves: 10-12 as a side dish

Sweet Potato Pie

Submitted by Richard B. McConnell

1½ cups	boiled sweet potatoes
2	eggs, separated
¾ cup	brown sugar
2 cups	milk
2 Tablespoons	butter, melted
1 teaspoon	nutmeg or cinnamon
½ teaspoon	baking powder
	pinch of salt

Mash boiled potatoes. Beat egg yolks with sugar, add to potatoes with milk, melted butter and spice. Fold in well-beaten egg whites, baking powder and salt. Pour into a pastry-lined pie pan. Bake until a silver knife inserted in center comes out clean, about 45 minutes in a 350° oven. **Serves: 8**

The Battle of New Orleans

Submitted by Lillian Negueloua

Jean Lafitte was known to many as a villainous pirate who, with his men, would raid and terrorize any boat in the Gulf of Mexico as it approached the mouth of the Mississippi and came towards New Orleans. In the Battle of New Orleans, however, Lafitte became a hero as he and his men helped Andrew Jackson defeat the British. It is said that Lafitte, Jackson and their troops stopped the raid of the British bullets with bales of cotton, which they piled into a thick wall.

"Battle of New Orleans" Bread Pudding A La Bouillie

Submitted by Janet Chouest

1	**French bread**
2 cups	**sugar**
8	**eggs**
½ teaspoon	**salt**
½ stick	**butter, melted**
½ teaspoon	**cinnamon**
2 cups	**evaporated milk**
1 cup	**dried brown raisins, soaked in hot water and drained**
3 teaspoons	**vanilla**
1 small can (6 ounces)	**crushed pineapple (with juice)**
1 cup	**fruit cocktail (with juice)**
½ cup	**flaked coconut**
3	**bananas, mashed**

A La Bouillie:

½ gallon	milk
2 cans (26 ounces total)	evaporated milk
6	eggs
2 Tablespoons	vanilla
1½ cups	sugar
¼ cup	water
6 Tablespoons	cornstarch
½ cup	toasted coconut

Break bread into small pieces and place in large bowl, cover with water and soak 5 minutes. Then strain and put back into bowl. Add sugar, eggs, salt, butter and cinnamon and mix well. Add remaining ingredients and mix very well. Grease 13 × 9-inch pan and bake in 350° oven for 1 hour. Pour A La Bouillie over bread pudding.

For A La Bouillie, bring milk and evaporated milk to a boil. In a separate bowl beat eggs, vanilla and sugar, mix water with cornstarch, add cornstarch mixture to egg mixture, reduce heat. Gradually stir mixture into hot milk. Stirring constantly, cook until thick and pour over bread pudding, garnish with toasted coconut. **Serves:** 8 or more

The Loup-garoux of Bayou Goula

Werewolves or "loup-garoux" were summoned up by Acadian and Creole mothers in imaginary stories intended to keep rebellious children in line. The Louisiana loup-garou, however, apparently suffered a seachange and was never as fearsome as in the stories told about him in his native Europe. All our local loup-garoux are now said to appear only once a year at an annual reunion on the banks of Bayou Goula, near Plaquemines and White Castle, at midnight of the first Sunday after the first full moon in April.

"Bayou" Cold Shrimp Soup (La Soupe Froide De Crevettes)

Submitted By Chef Michel Marcais, La Fete, 1984

18 ounces	shrimp, headed
1	onion
1 cup	white wine
2 Tablespoons	flour
2	egg whites
2 cups	heavy cream
	salt and pepper
½ bunch	watercress

Peel shrimp. Sauté shrimp shells with chopped onion, white wine, and flour and stir. Add water to the top. Cook 30 minutes and then strain.

Add 9 ounces of the shrimp to the stock and cook for 3 minutes. Keep cold in six soup bowls.

Take the remaining shrimp and put in blender, adding egg whites, 1 cup of the cream, salt and pepper. Mix well. From this mixture, make 18 dumplings and poach gently. Place 3 dumplings on each soup plate.

Chop the watercress very fine. Whip the remaining heavy cream and add to watercress. Make 1 rosette on each plate. **Serves:** 6

The Legend of Spanish Moss

A young Acadian returns to the oak tree where he would frequently meet his love to find that his fiancée died of a broken heart during his absence. There he sees suspended a lock of his true love's hair. The lock, symbolic of fidelity and love, was transformed miraculously into Spanish moss.

Caldo—Spanish Soup

Submitted by Louise Perez

1 pound	white beans
3 medium	onions, chopped
1 can (16 ounces)	stewed tomatoes
1 can (15 ounces)	tomato sauce
5 pieces	1-inch thick pickled pork
1 package (10 ounces)	frozen lima beans
1 pound	fresh snap beans, or 2 (8 ounces each) packages of frozen snap beans
1 large	turnip, cut into pieces
6	carrots
1 large package	(20 ounces) frozen mixed vegetables
1 can (15 ounces)	white corn
1 can (15 ounces)	green peas
6 pieces	corn on the cob
6	red potatoes (Irish potatoes)
1 small	head cabbage
½ package (5 ounces total)	frozen mustard greens
6	sweet potatoes salt and pepper to taste

Put white beans in large pot. Fill pot half full of water. Add onions, stewed tomatoes and tomato sauce. When beans are half tender, cut pickled pork in pieces and add to beans. When meat is tender, add lima beans, snap beans, turnip, carrots and frozen mixed vegetables. After it comes to a full boil again, add a can of whole corn, a can of peas, pieces of corn on cob and Irish potatoes. Then add cabbage cut in small pieces and mustard greens. When everything is tender turn off heat.

When soup is cooking take some of stock from soup or just put enough water in another small pot. Cook sweet potatoes until tender. (The reason for that is if you put sweet potatoes with soup, they tend to break apart.) Add sweet potatoes to soup pot. If soup gets a little thick, add some water because it is supposed to be a little soupy. Salt and pepper to taste. (Taste before adding salt because the meat will be a little salty.) **Serves:** 10-12

Aunt Julie's Paella

Submitted by Chiqui Collier, Cookery N'Orleans Style Restaurant

This is one of my favorite dishes to prepare when a crowd is coming over for dinner. It makes a beautiful presentation and flavor is simply divine!

1	chicken cut-up or 4 thighs and 4 legs
	salt and pepper to taste
1 pound	lean pork, cut into 1-inch cubes
1 medium	onion, minced
2 large toes	garlic, minced

Cut into 1½-inch julienne strips:

½ large	bell pepper,
1 large	carrot,
1 piece	celery

1 cup	frozen green peas
1½ pounds	peeled shrimp
⅓ (4 ounce size) jar	sliced pimento
2 teaspoons	capers with juice
½ (8 ounce size) jar	pimento stuffed olives (green)
½ pound	calamari (squid), cleaned and sliced
5 cups	water
4	chicken bouillon cubes
1 teaspoon	saffron threads
2½ cups	Uncle Ben's® rice (raw)
3	hard boiled eggs, sliced
½ pound	unpeeled shrimp (heads on)
	oil for frying

In a large electric skillet or paella pan, brown chicken pieces that have been seasoned with salt and pepper in a little oil. Remove from pan. In drippings add pork cubes and brown 5 minutes. Remove from pan. In pan drippings (add a little more oil if necessary) add onions, garlic, bell pepper, celery and carrot. Stir fry 2 minutes. Add peas, peeled shrimp, pimentos, capers, olives, chicken, calamari, and pork. Stir. In a separate pot, bring the 5 cups of water to a boil. Stir in bouillon cubes and saffron. Let it stand 5 minutes until dissolved. Gently stir in rice to skillet mixture. Slowly pour in enough bouillon mixture to cover rice and chicken pieces. Cover and cook on low fire about 20 minutes. Uncover and decoratively arrange egg slices and raw unpeeled shrimp. (Add more broth as necessary to keep rice moist.) Cover and steam another 10 minutes until shrimp are cooked and rice is tender. (Paella should be moist but not wet!) Place pan on a hot pad on the serving table and let everyone help themselves.

Serve with a mixed green salad, red ripe tomatoes and some French bread.

Also mix up a pitcher of Sangria and enjoy!
Serves: 12

The Ghost of St. Louis Cemetery

Submitted by Liz A. Steil

New Orleans Cab Drivers avoid St. Louis Cemetery #1 whenever possible. One night a cabbie picked up a beautiful teenage girl. She was cold so he loaned her his jacket. He dropped her off with instructions to return to the same house in one hour. When he returned, he waited for a while, and when the girl did not come out, he went to the house to inquire about his passenger. When he described the young girl to the man who answered the door, he exclaimed, "That's my daughter. She's been dead for years." When the cabbie asked about the jacket, the man told him his poor daughter was buried in Old St. Louis #1, and it was impossible for her to have the jacket. The cabbie returned to the cemetery and found the girl's tomb exactly where her father described, with his jacket folded neatly on top.

"Ghostly" Gratin of Pumpkin

Submitted by Gerard Crozier, Crozier's Restaurant

This is a good way to use the pumpkins you have decorated (but not cut up) at Halloween time. For the past 10 years, this vegetable has been served at Crozier's during Halloween week, but it is also a delicious winter vegetable so do not limit yourself to Halloween.

1	**pumpkin (big enough to yield one cup of puréed pumpkin)**
½ cup	**very thick bechamel sauce**
	salt, pepper (white) to taste
½ cup	**grated swiss cheese**
1 Tablespoon	**butter**

Peel pumpkin and cook in salted water until tender. Drain overnight (this is very important otherwise dish is too watery). Make a very thick bechamel sauce to which you add ½ the swiss cheese. Press the pumpkin through a food mill then sauté it in 1 tablespoon butter (this is to further dry it out). Mix pumpkin with bechamel sauce, then salt and pepper to taste. Pour in buttered gratin dish. Sprinkle remainder of swiss cheese on top. Bake in 450° oven until cheese is brown. **Serves: 4**

The Haunted House

Courtesy of Riverwalk

There is a house on the corner of Royal and St. Ann Streets that is reputed to be one of the haunted houses in the Vieux Carré. There are those who swear that on a wintry night, the naked figure of a woman walking up on the roof and shivering and wringing her hands was seen. Tradition has identified her as a beautiful quadroon who fell in love with her white master. When she revealed her love to him, he told her that he would become her lover if she would walk naked on the roof top all that night—the coldest in the year. To prove her love and obedience, the girl climbed the roof shortly after dark and complied with the master's stipulations. She was so frozen by midnight that she could no longer move and fell into a coma from which she never awoke. Those who know about such phenomena say that she is still walking and waiting.

"Midnight" Strawberry Royal

Submitted by Ann Davis

An exciting, delightful dessert for all occasions.

½ cup	pecans, coarsely chopped
1 cup	flour, plain
⅓ cup	brown sugar, light
½ cup	butter, melted

Mix together ingredients and spread in 9-inch × 13-inch pan. Bake at 350° for 20 minutes. Stir mixture often while in the oven. Remove pan from oven and cool. Remove ⅓ of mixture for topping. Spread remaining ⅔ of mixture in bottom of same pan.

Strawberry filling:

4	egg whites
½ cup	sugar
3 teaspoons	lemon juice
20	fresh or frozen strawberries, chopped
1 carton (12 ounces)	whipped topping

Beat egg whites until peaks form. Add sugar slowly. Fold in lemon juice and strawberries and mix thoroughly. Fold in whipped topping. Spread mixture over the crumb crust and top with remaining crumbs. Cover and freeze for 6 hours. Remove and let stand for 20 minutes before cutting.
Serves: 12

The Legend of the Creole Queen

Submitted by the Creole Queen

If you happen to be strolling the decks of the Creole Queen late on a dark moonless night, you may witness an unusual phenomena—the ghostly apparition of a beautiful Creole woman who seems to be waiting for someone. Many have seen her and say she is Vivienne Laveaux, related to Marie Laveaux, the woman who held sway over voodoo in New Orleans for over 70 years in the late 1800s.

The story of Vivienne begins sometime near the end of New Orleans' "golden era"—the period from 1825 to the beginning of the Civil War. It was then that money flowed easily throughout the city, glamorous floating palaces churned their way up and down the Mississippi and wealthy merchants and planters gave balls and banquets almost nightly.

At this time, there appeared in New Orleans an impeccably dressed gentleman known only as M. Croix. He was slightly-built, dark, and with entrancing eyes that could, some say, read the very depths of one's soul. He was as handy with a rapier as he was with the cards, and it wasn't long before he made a reputation for himself on both counts with the wealthy young Creoles of the city.

Wearying of the young bucks and their pompous attitudes, however, Croix soon sought new territory and began plying the gaming tables of the Mississippi's grand steamboats. Skillfully he parlayed winning after winning into a small fortune, which often made him the target of speculative businessmen seeking a "partner" for their ventures.

One of these solicitors was a M. Villere. He was a builder of steamboats looking for a primary investor for a new vessel he was contemplating. At first M. Croix couldn't be bothered, but one evening M.

Villere came to his table for one last try. He was accompanied by his mistress, a beautiful enchanting Creole woman named Vivienne Laveux. M. Croix could hardly keep his eyes off her and paid little if any attention to M. Villere and his ramblings. Finally, he waved M. Villere quiet and indicated he would invest.

The steamboat was built and M. Croix, as its principal investor, decided to name it Creole Queen for Vivienne. Unbeknownst to M. Villere a secret intrigue had grown between Vivienne and M. Croix which, however, would not remain secret for long. M. Croix, confident in his position, began to openly escort Vivienne on cruises of the Queen. She was his luck at the gambling tables.

One oddity that M. Croix exhibited was that every now and again he would disappear, sometimes for weeks, with no explanation. But he always reassured Vivienne that she need only wait for him aboard the Creole Queen and he would return.

M. Villere noted the goings on between the two lovers. It incensed him! He also was aware of M. Croix's mysterious trips. A devious idea occured to him. He would arrange for M. Croix to take a permanent "trip." With this in mind, he held a clandestine meeting with several thugs on one of the back streets of the Vieux Carré and paid them well.

Several days later M. Croix was gone. Two days after that, strangely enough, one of the thugs met with M. Villere to inquire when M. Croix would return—they had been unable to set up the "kill."

Weeks turned into months and M. Croix did not return. M. Villere soon forgot about him, but Vivienne became despondent, spending more and more time walking the decks of the Creole Queen waiting. . .M. Villere tried everything to win his mistress' favor back, but she would have none of it, returning only ridicule and scorn. This so enraged him that one moonless night he strangled Vivienne and threw her body overboard.

From that night onward, bad luck plague

Queen—and several months later the ship was nearly destroyed during the early months of the Civil War. She was stripped of all her finery and all the salvageable material, which included navigational fittings, brass fixtures from salons and staterooms, intricately carved woodwork and paneling and was purchased by a dealer in Vicksburg, Mississippi. It lay stored, gathering dust in an obscure warehouse for years. It wasn't until the late seventies that it was discovered by the builder of the present Creole Queen, who used many items from the original steamboat in the new one.

Some say that the use of these original parts accounts for the unusual apparition observed from time to time on the decks of the present Creole Queen, which by the way, docks at the Riverwalk in almost the same location as the original steamboat did.

Has Vivienne Laveaux "followed" the parts of the old Queen to continue her vigil. . .to await the return of her lover?

"Creole Queen" Seafood Okra Gumbo

Submitted by The Gumbo Shop

The Gumbo Shop, official caterer of the Creole Queen, makes this wonderful recipe daily aboard the river cruises.

2-3 pounds	shrimp
2 quarts	water
2 Tablespoons	oil
1 quart	okra (cut into ½-inch pieces)
⅔ cup	oil
½ cup	flour

2 medium	onions chopped
1	bell pepper chopped
2 ribs	celery chopped
2 cloves	garlic chopped
¼ cup	parsley
1 can (16 ounces)	stewed tomatoes
2 small	boiled crabs
2	bay leaves
2 Tablespoons	Worcestershire sauce
½ teaspoon	black pepper
½ teaspoon	cayenne pepper
	salt to taste

Peel and devein shrimp. Set aside in refrigerator. Boil shrimp shells in 2 quarts water for several hours to make a stock. Set aside.

In a heavy skillet, heat 2 tablespoons oil and sauté the okra until all ropiness is gone, about ½ hour. Set aside.

In large (6-8 quart) heavy Dutch oven, make a dark brown roux with the oil and flour. Add chopped onions, bell pepper, celery, garlic and parsley and sauté until tender. Add tomatoes and cook 15 minutes. Add sauteéd okra, shrimp stock, crabs (broken in quarters), bay leaves, Worcestershire sauce, black pepper and cayenne pepper. Bring to a slow boil and simmer for about 2 hours, stirring occasionally. Add salt to taste. Add the peeled shrimp and continue cooking until shrimp are done.

Serve over steamed rice. This dish is best if cooked a day in in advance and refrigerated overnight. **Serves:** 8 or more

The Legend of Ah-tee

Reprinted from the play "A Bilingual Celebration," published by Swallow Publishing Company. Submitted by Pierre V. Daigle, Author and Songwriter

There is a legend among us, the Acadians. The Legend of Ah-tee. Being the first child born in old Acadia, Canada, Ahtee was the first Acadian woman.

Ah-tee grew up to be a fine and beautiful woman. In time she married and raised a family. When Ah-tee was very old, God appeared before her and announced that He would create on earth a symbol of Ah-tee's faithfulness, her cheerful disposition, and her attributes as a homemaker. And so it was that God created the meadow lark. He decreed that forever would the children of the lark be dressed as follows: On the back of each lark would be worn a shawl of black and brown colors, and those colors would be draped over a field of white. This is the exact replica of the shawl Ah-tee wore over a white dress while she went about visiting her sick or despondent neighbors. The white areas between the brown and black markings stand for the purity of mothers' hearts the world over. The brown markings represent the stresses and difficulties of motherhood; the black markings on the lark's back stand for the many small tragedies that are invariably in the experience of all mothers.

Now, thought the Lord, this symbol must wear a great area of yellow. Yellow because it was Ah-tee's favorite color, and even more importantly, it will stand for her wish that the symbol of herself should represent the love and joy in the hearts of mothers.

After dressing the lark in a yellow dress from her throat to her legs, there still seemed to be something missing. The great area of yellow was beautiful. It stood for the universal love that mothers have for their children. It stood for faith, and for love of God, but still something was missing.

Suddenly, God knew what was missing. He placed

a special mark around the throat of the lark. This mark is in the form of a blazer of solid black. This striking black mark would forever stand as a reminder to all humankind of how close to tragedy a mother's heart is. The Lord always knows that a mother's heart, after her first time of giving birth, can never again stand alone. She can never withdraw from the life she has created. No matter how many children she has—no matter how far they wander, her heart always goes with them.

Having given the lark all the markings that would be symbols of Ah-tee and of all mothers forever, God proceeded to endow the lark with the many other attributes of Ah-tee, the first Acadian woman. In memory of Ah-tee's skills as a homemaker, God made the lark the most skillful and most meticulous nest builder of all birds. Carefully, and neatly, and quietly, except for her occasional song, the lark weaves a canopy of grass among the sweet clovers of meadows. Carefully she tends her nest, and she is at all times, a solicitious mother to her children. And each year the lark is the first to sing the arrival of spring, forever symbolizing the love of mothers who bring new generations to humankind. And throughout spring, summer, and even fall, the lark sings for humankind her cheerful, halfwhistle, halfvoiced song.

In winter the lark is silent. Her silence is a mournful reminder of the death of Ah-tee, the first Acadian woman, and of the deaths of all mothers since the beginning of time on earth.

Other titles by Pierre V. Daigle: Tears, Love and Laughter *and* Plow, Sword and Prayers. *Mr. Daigle also writes songs for "Cajun Gold."*

Cajun Crabmeat and Shrimp Au Gratin

Submitted by Chiqui Collier, Cookery N'Orleans Style Restaurant

2 sticks	butter
1 bunch	green onions
1½ pounds	peeled shrimp
	salt and lemon pepper to taste or ¼ to ½ teaspoon Creole seasoning®
1½ pounds	lump crabmeat
¼ cup	flour
1½ cups	heavy cream
¼ cup	dry sherry (optional)
1 cup	chicken bouillon
1 Tablespoon	Lea & Perrins® Worcestershire
dash	Tabasco® (optional)
¼ cup	parmesan cheese
1 cup	grated cheddar cheese

In a large nonstick skillet, melt 1 stick butter. Add green onions and shrimp. Cook 2 minutes. Season with salt and lemon pepper or the Creole seasoning to taste. Fold in crabmeat, being careful not to break up the lumps. Spread mixture over the bottom of 2-quart Pyrex dish. In the same skillet, melt the second stick of butter. Stir in flour. Cook 3 minutes. Stir in cream, sherry and bouillon. Simmer on low heat 5 minutes until thickened. Stir in Lea & Perrins, Tabasco and parmesan cheese. Pour over seafood. Top with grated cheese. Bake at 350° for 20 minutes. **Variation:** This can also be prepared in individual casserole dishes or ramekins. **Serves:** 6-8

Pork Medallions Zatarain

Submitted by Al Copeland, Copeland's of New Orleans

3 pounds	pork loin, boned, sliced ½-inch thick
1 Tablespoon	salt
1 Tablespoon	cayenne pepper
1 Tablespoon	white pepper
2 cups	flour
½ cup	butter
2 quarts	cream
6 ounces	Zatarain Creole mustard®
	salt to taste
	Tabasco® to taste

Pound pork pieces until thin. Mix salt, cayenne, white pepper and flour in a bag until well blended. Pour into shallow container. Dust pork pieces in seasoned flour and sauté in butter quickly, about 1 minute for both sides. Hold in warm oven.

For sauce: (May be done ahead of time.) Bring cream to a boil. Reduce heat and simmer until thickened, about 20 minutes. Add mustard, salt, and Tabasco. Ladle sauce into plate. Place pork medallions on sauce. Add additional sauce. **Serves:** 6-8

Andouille In Puff Pastry Appetizers

Submitted by Al Copeland, Copeland's of New Orleans

The combination of flavors and textures makes this a special dish, perfect to accompany any hearty meal.

1 large,	fresh andouille sausage (about 1¾ pounds) Puff Pastry (prepared pastry or filo pastry, available in the frozen or refrigerated department of grocery or specialty store Creole mustard
1 cup	grated cheddar cheese
1	egg white

To cook the sausage, slit the skin at several points with a knife to keep it from splitting while cooking. Place in a pot of cold water and bring to a boil. Turn down the heat and simmer for 45 minutes. Remove, allow to cool on a cloth, then carefully remove skin with a knife. Chop coarsely.

Preheat oven to 425°. Spread puff pastry sheets as directed. Cut into 4-inch squares. Place a tablespoon of andouille in center of each square. For variety, place a dollop of Creole mustard on ⅓ of the appetizers, 2 tablespoons grated cheese on ⅓ and leave ⅓ plain.

Brush edges with beaten egg white, fold into triangle and press edges together with fork to seal and flute. Brush tops with beaten egg white. Bake at 425° for about 15 minutes or until golden brown. **Variation:** Fresh pork or Italian sausage may be substituted for the andouille sausage. **Serves: 8**

Marinated Crab Fingers

Submitted by Nicole Ferrier, Ralph & Kacoo's Restaurant

32	cooked crab claws
1 cup	olive oil
½ cup	red wine vinegar
¼ cup	lemon juice
1 teaspoon	tarragon leaves
10 cloves	garlic, minced
1 cup	green onion, chopped
1 cup	parsley, chopped
1 cup	celery, chopped
¾ teaspoon	salt
¾ teaspoon	sugar
¾ teaspoon	black pepper

Crack crab claws and remove half of shell. Set aside. Mix remaining ingredients and refrigerate. When ready to serve, place crab claws on serving platter and pour marinade over them. **Serves: 8**

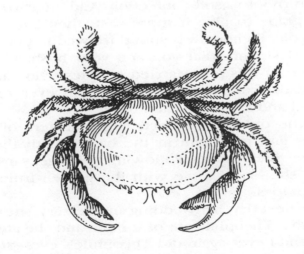

The Legend of Mattie's Pie
(Mattie is pronounced Mah Taý)

Submitted by Pierre V. Daigle, Author and Songwriter

In the early days, soon after the first Acadians arrived in southwest Louisiana, Mattie Doucet, wife of Theophile Doucet, learned her husband was falling in love with another woman.

Heartbroken and feeling helpless, she went into a grove of trees to pray, to weep, and to wonder at the cruel fate of life. On a grassy clearing between tall trees she knelt, raised her eyes to Heaven and prayed, "Oh, God! I have been a good and loving wife. Why should I suffer the cruel fate of having to walk alone on this earth?

Almost instantly an angel appeared before Mattie. In a beautiful basket made of woven strips of wood she carried ten vine peaches. "Take these vine peaches," said the angel. "Cook them in honey until they turn into a soft confection. Add juice from the wild grape to give it more zest, then bake them into a pie. Tomorrow is your third wedding anniversary. Make sure that you and your husband eat a portion of this pie. Married couples who eat of a pie made from the vine peach will ever remain faithful and loving to each other."

Mattie quickly gathered large clusters of wild grapes and put them in the basket with the ten golden vine peaches. Following the angel's instructions, she baked a pie with the golden fruits and wild grapes.

The next day, her wedding anniversary, she made sure that Theophile ate of the pie and she ate of it also, and never again did Theophile's eyes stray to the face of another woman.

Naturally, Mattie, while peeling and slicing the ten vine peaches, was careful to save every seed, and every spring thereafter she grew a crop of her own vine peaches. She also provided seeds to the other Acadians. As the legend of Mattie's pie with the magical powers to instill love and faithfulness spread, so did the popularity of the golden fruit known as vine peaches spread. In time, it became a tradition among Acadian wives and mothers to bake vine peach pies, not only on their anniversaries, but also on their children's birthdays.

Acadian Peach Pie

Submitted by Gerry Vince

	milk
1 quart	fresh peaches (washed, peeled, sliced)
1 cup	sugar
¼ cup	cornstarch
1 Tablespoon	lemon juice
2 Tablespoons	butter
	pinch of salt
	9-inch pie shell, baked and cooled
	whipped cream

Pour a little milk over fruit slices to prevent fruit from darkening. Mash 1 cup of peaches, cook in small amount of water (approximately ¾ cup) for 5 minutes. Mix sugar and cornstarch into the mashed peaches. Cook until thick and clear. Add lemon juice, butter and salt and let cool. Arrange remaining fruit in pie shell and pour cooled fruit mixture over pie. Serve with whipped cream. **Serves:** 8

Peach Dumplings

Submitted by Mrs. Lester F. Alexander, Sr.

	sufficient pie crust for 6 dumplings
2½ cups	fresh peaches, sliced
1 Tablespoon	lemon juice
½ cup	sugar
1 Tablespoon	butter
½ teaspoon	cinnamon

Mix above ingredients except pie crust and divide into six parts. Place one part on each of 6 pastry squares. Bring pastry together to make dumpling. Place in greased baking pan and bake in oven at 350° until brown, about 10 minutes. Baste with sauce, and bake about 20 minutes longer.

Sauce:

2	peaches, sliced
2 cups	water
½ cup	sugar
2 Tablespoons	butter
½ teaspoon	cinnamon

Cook until peaches are soft. Mash through sieve. Baste peach dumplings with sauce. **Yield:** 6 dumplings with sauce

My Cousin Pete

Submitted by Abe Ritman, Abe's Sea & Sirloin Restaurant

Papa Schexniche had a fine 16 year old son named Peter, thin and real long; 84 inches long. We never knew how tall he was, 'cause nobody could reach that high. So he would have to lay on the floor and we would know how long he was, 84 inches long.

He was so thin that Papa Schexniche would use Peter as a pole to push along the pirogue. He had to quit when Peter tangled with some mean alligators. That's when Peter got his new name; we now call him Pete for short.

Pirogue Pancakes

Submitted by Mrs. Carl F. Dahlberg, Sr.

3	eggs
	pinch salt
1 cup	sweet milk
¾ cup	sifted plain white flour
	butter

Separate eggs, placing yolks in mixing bowl. Add salt. Add milk and flour alternately to make a batter, which will be quite thin. Beat the whites and fold in. Drop the cakes on a buttered griddle from a large spoon and bake to a nice brown, turning first on one side and then on the other. **Yield:** 10 or more pancakes

Voodoo

Submitted by Mildred L. Covert and Sylvia P. Gerson

Congo Square, on the present site of Armstrong Park, was where the slaves and free men of color were allowed to congregate on Sunday evenings. They brought with them the practice of Voodoo. The Square was the scene of such dances as the "calinda"—a sensuous African dance where men and women faced each other. Participants also danced the "bamboula" to the beat of a drum made of bamboo.

In the early 1800s the devotees of Voodoo worshipped a snake in secret rites concluding with frenzied dancing. Marie Laveaux, best known of the voodoo queens, was a hairdresser. She exerted much power among the superstitious members of her race and among many white people, who sought both her advice and the gris-gris (pronounced gree-gree) she sold. These were charms or amulets for good or evil. Many were concoctions of salt, gunpowder, saffron, and dried dog dung. Gris-gris balls as large as oranges were made from brightly colored feathers. Some gris-gris were secreted in a pillow or a bed. Others, such as a cross of wet salt, were placed on the doorstep and meant trouble for the recipient (a small coffin on the gallery meant death). A favorite good luck gris-gris was a dime with a hole in it worn around the ankle. There were love potions, moneymaking incense, "boss-fixing" potions, the black candle, and the famous pin-ridden Voodoo doll.

The Voodoo cult continues to exist today. Whether fact or fiction, mysticism and tales surrounding Voodooism still abound, fascinating natives and visitors alike.

"Good Luck" Rice Custard

Submitted by Louise Perez

1½ cups	raw rice
4 cups	water
1½ cups	sugar
2 cans (5 ounces each)	evaporated milk
½ cup	raisins
½ box (3 ounce size)	vanilla pudding
5	eggs, separated
1 teaspoon	vanilla
	cinnamon to taste

Cook rice in 4 cups water, add sugar and cook until almost tender. Add evaporated milk, raisins and mix pudding mix in a cup of milk. Add to rice. Beat egg whites until stiff. Beat yolks separately and then mix whites and yolks together. When rice is tender add vanilla, cinnamon and egg mixture. Then turn off heat. Mix well. If it seems a little thick just add some more milk. **Serves:** 6 or more

The Legend of Martha

Courtesy of Riverwalk

Once upon a time under a great oak tree two gentlemen faced each other in a duel for a young lady's hand in marriage. The two suitors who were owners of neighboring River Road plantations upstream from New Orleans, fought hand-to-hand until finally one conceded to the other.

Happy with the way the victory had fallen, the young lady soon wed her gentleman. They spent many joyous, prosperous years working the land and raising their two sons. But even with the passage of time, the hatred between the neighboring families did not abate, and was passed on to their children.

Upon the father's death, the older of the two sons inherited the land. The younger son, with a large monetary inheritance, left for the thriving port city of New Orleans where he established himself as a merchant and later married. Only one child was born to him—a daughter Martha, upon whom he lavished every comfort and luxury.

By her eighteenth summer Martha had become a beautiful young woman and went to visit her cousins on their plantation. Alone one afternoon on a carriage stroll through country lanes, she felt a wheel loosen beneath the buggy. Fortunately, a young gentleman on a fine horse soon happened upon her and repaired the wheel.

The sun was setting as he took the reins of the carriage to see her safely home. Along the way, they talked and laughed easily, feeling comfortable and happy in each other's company.

When Martha arrived at her cousins' home, she was sternly admonished for even speaking to her rescuer. Unknown to her, he was owner of the neighboring plantation and grandson of the man who had dueled with her grandfather.

Nevertheless, the young lady and her suitor managed to meet several times during the summer, and fell in love. When they were discovered, Martha was sent back to New Orleans, but not before one more rendezvous had been arranged.

Early one morning she walked to the French Market, and there she met her gentleman. Amid the crowd of fruit and vegetable vendors and the throng of customers, they talked while she filled her basket with produce from his plantation: red ripe strawberries, sweet bell peppers, mirlitons, and okra. Then, he took her hand and proposed marriage, asking her to come live with him on his plantation. Wanting so desperately to say "yes," Martha nevertheless dreaded the consequences of the union. She would be banished forever from her family, bring heartache to her doting father, and create a rift between him and her uncle.

Pulling her hand away, she turned and left the market quickly, her heart breaking as she did so.

But as Martha walked along the river through the French Market Alley, she pondered the prospect of a life without the man she loved. Unable to go another step without a decision, she sat down on a nearby wrought iron bench, the basket of produce cradled in her lap to make her choice.

Martha's magical presence lingers there still, her image captured forever in a bronze sculpture by New Orleans artist Paul Perret in the French Market Alley between the Levee and Decatur Street.

Poised on her bench, Martha ponders her dilemma amid the bustle of modern-day New Orleans. The exquisite craftsmanship of the sculpture is evident from the fine detail of the young lady's face to the mouthwatering realism of the Louisiana produce she holds, affording passersby a brief encounter with a New Orleans long since gone.

French Market Doughnuts (Billie's Beignets)

Submitted by Billie Cleaver

¾ cup	evaporated milk (undiluted from can)
½ cup	sugar
½ cup	butter
¾ teaspoon	salt
½ cup	warm water
1 package	active dry yeast
1	egg (extra large)
4½ cups	flour
	oil for frying
	confectioners sugar

Combine evaporated milk, sugar, butter and salt in saucepan. Heat until butter is melted. Cool to lukewarm. Put warm water into large bowl and sprinkle in yeast; stir until completely dissolved. Add lukewarm milk mixture and egg. Beat in 2 cups of the flour. Add enough of the rest of the flour to make a dough.

Turn on a floured board. Knead until smooth and elastic (about 8 minutes). Put dough in large greased bowl and cover with a damp towel and let rise in a warm place until double in size (about 2 hours). Punch dough down on floured board and knead. Roll out to a rectangle (about ¼-inch thick). Cut into 2½ inch squares, cover with a towel and let rise ½ hour or until doubled.

Heat oil in a deep fryer to 375°. Fry beignets a few at a time until puffed and golden brown (about 3 minutes) turning once. Drain. While warm, sprinkle generously with confectioners sugar. **Yield:** approximately 3 dozen beignets

Shrimp and Crab Okra Gumbo

Submitted by The Bon Ton Café

1 cup	flour
1 cup	vegetable oil
4 cups	chopped okra
2 cups	large onions, diced
½ cup	bell pepper, diced
½ cup	green onions (shallots), chopped
½ cup	celery, diced
3 Tablespoons	garlic cloves, chopped
6 quarts	water
4	gumbo crabs (cleaned and cut in half)
1 Tablespoon	tomato paste
2 pounds	peeled shrimp (60-70 count) salt and pepper to taste
½ cup	chopped parsley parsley for garnish

Make a roux by mixing flour in hot oil and stirring constantly using a thick frying pan. Stir until roux is golden brown (use low-medium flame). Put aside. Smother okra in side pot in ½ quart of water until thick and mushy. Place on side. Sauté onions, bell pepper, green onions, and celery and garlic until limp in cooking oil in gumbo pot. Add roux to seasoning and stir until well mixed. Add 6 quarts water and bring to boil. Add smothered okra, crab and tomato paste and allow to simmer 1 hour on medium flame stirring occasionally to prevent burning. Add shrimp, salt and pepper and simmer 1 more hour. Gumbo should be slightly thickened. Sprinkle parsley and serve on steamed rice.
Serves: a crowd!

Crabmeat Raviogoté

*Submitted by Anthony DiPiazza, Chef Du Maison,
Pascal's Manale Restaurant*

A tantalizing appetizer served usually during the Christmas and Easter Holidays, preceding a dinner consisting of beef or pork entrées.

1 cup	bell peppers, chopped
½ cup	pimento peppers, chopped
½ cup	mushrooms, sliced
½ cup	green onions, chopped
⅛ cup	parsley
	salt and pepper to taste
½ cup	butter
1 pound	lump crabmeat
	bread crumbs

Sauté all ingredients except crabmeat and bread crumbs in ¼ cup butter. Add lump crabmeat and cook 10 minutes. Dish into four casseroles (or ramekins), dust with bread crumbs and drizzle with ¼ cup melted butter. Brown under a hot flame. **Serves: 4**

Summer Squash Casserole

Submitted by Mary Michael

1 pound	summer squash
1 cup	grated cheddar cheese
1 medium	onion, chopped
2	beaten eggs
3 Tablespoons	melted butter
1 teaspoon	sage
1 Tablespoon	sugar
	paprika

Cook squash and drain. Mix with ½ cup of cheese, onion, eggs, butter, sage and sugar. Place in buttered baking dish. Top with remaining cheese and paprika. Bake at 400° for 20 to 25 minutes. **Serves:** 6-8

La Compote De Mirliton Aux Fraises (Mirliton Compote with Strawberries)

Submitted by Chef Michel Marcais, La Fête 1984

6	mirlitons
3 cups	sugar
	dash vanilla extract
	dash sugar
2 cups	heavy cream
6	egg yolks
	dash kirsh

Peel and seed mirlitons. Cook until tender, covered in water and ½ cup sugar. Remove from water. Cool and slice lengthwise.

Blend half of the mirlitons with vanilla and dash of sugar to taste.

Blend cream and egg yolks in double boiler over low heat, slowly whipping until thick. Add remaining 1½ cups sugar and kirsh.

Place a scoop of mirliton purée on plate and top with sliced mirliton and fan design. Surround with strawberries and top with sauce. **Serves:** 6

Trout with Roasted Pecans

Submitted by Commander's Palace Restaurant

Pecan Butter:

1 cup	shelled pecans
½ stick (4 Tablespoons)	unsalted butter, softened
	juice of ½ medium lemon
1 teaspoon	Worcestershire sauce

Creole Meuniere Sauce:

2 Tablespoons	cooking oil
2 Tablespoons	all purpose flour
1½ cups	fish stock
	salt and freshly ground black pepper to taste
1 stick (8 Tablespoons)	unsalted butter, cut into chunks and softened
2 Tablespoons	Worcestershire sauce
	juice of 1 lemon
¼ cup	chopped parsley

Sautéed Trout:

2 medium	eggs, lightly beaten
1 cup	milk
2 teaspoons	Creole seafood seasoning
1 cup	all purpose flour
6	trout fillets (6 ounces each)
½ cup	clarified butter or half cooking oil and half margarine

Garnish:

½ cup	reserved chopped roasted pecans
	parsley sprigs
	lemon wedges

Spread pecans on a cookie sheet and bake in a preheated 350° oven for 10 minutes. Coarsely chop half the roasted pecans and set aside for garnish. Put remaining half into container of a blender or food processor. Add butter, lemon juice, and Worcestershire sauce and blend to a smooth butter. Set aside.

To make sauce: heat oil in a heavy skillet. Remove from heat and add flour. Return to heat and cook, stirring, until the roux becomes medium brown in color. Slowly whisk in stock, bring to a boil, stirring constantly, and simmer for 45 minutes. Add salt and pepper to taste. There should be about 1 cup sauce.

Transfer the brown fish sauce to a 2-quart saucepan and bring back to a quick simmer. Whisk in softened butter and Worcestershire sauce and continue to whisk until butter is absorbed. Add lemon juice and parsley. Whisk again briefly and remove from heat. This sauce should be used within 45 minutes of the time it is completed.

To prepare trout: combine eggs and milk, beating until well blended. Set aside.

Combine seafood seasoning and flour on waxed paper or in an aluminum pie plate. Dredge fillets in the seasoned flour to coat them well on both sides, dip in egg-milk mixture, then again in the seasoned flour.

Melt clarified butter in a large skillet over medium-high heat. Lay fillets carefully in the pan and sauté quickly, turning only once, until crisp and golden brown on both sides, about 2 minutes per side. Remove to a warm serving platter.

To serve: Put a fillet on each plate and top with a heaping tablespoon of pecan butter, coating the entire fillet. Sprinkle with a heaping tablespoon of chopped roasted pecans. Cover trout and toppings with Creole meuniere sauce and garnish with parsley and lemon wedges. **Serves:** 6

Abe's Fable

Submitted by Abe Ritman, Abe's Sea & Sirloin Restaurant

When we opened our restaurant in Shreveport over thirty years ago, we were determined to feature the finest, freshest food in Louisiana. We got our oysters from Oyster Joe Martini and our bread from Angelo Gendusa on Rampart Street in New Orleans.

Even though the food was good, we felt like it lost something in the shipping. So, Angelo and myself set about trying to find a solution to the problem. One day, Angelo put the raw dough on the engines of his delivery trucks in New Orleans. By the time the trucks pulled into Shreveport, the rolls had not only risen to perfection, but were fully cooked. Hot and golden brown, they were ready for the table. Ever since that day Abe's has boasted of the freshest baked bread in Northern Louisiana.

Mimi's Bread Pudding

Submitted by Lois Comeaux

½ long	loaf stale French bread
1 can (12 ounces)	evaporated milk
12 ounces	water
3	beaten eggs
1-1½ cups	sugar
1 ounce	vanilla
½ cup	flour-dusted raisins
2 or 3	thinly sliced bananas

Whiskey sauce:

½ stick	butter
½ cup	sugar
1 jigger	whiskey or rum

Soak bread in evaporated milk and water for ½ hour.

Add eggs, sugar, vanilla, raisins and bananas. Bake at 350° for 45 minutes to 1 hour. Serve hot or cold with whiskey sauce.

For Whiskey sauce, warm ½ stick of butter and ½ cup sugar until melted. Add whiskey or rum. **Serves:** 4

French Bread

Submitted by Betty Comeaux

3 cups	unbleached white flour
2 packages	yeast
2½ cups	water
1 Tablespoon	sugar
1 Tablespoon	salt
1 Tablespoon	shortening
4-4½ cups	flour
	yellow cornmeal
1	egg white
1 Tablespoon	water

In large bowl combine flour and yeast, set aside. Heat 2½ cups water, sugar, salt and shortening until warm (not hot). Add to dry mixture. Beat with electric mixer on low for 1½ minutes and then 3 minutes on high. By hand, add flour to make a soft dough. Knead on floured surface 10-12 minutes. (Very important to knead the entire time.) Place in greased bowl, turn once, cover and let rise for 1-1½ hours. Punch down and divide in half. Cover and let rest 10 minutes. Roll each half into 15″ × 12″ rectangle. From long side, roll into log shape and seal well. Place each seam side down on greased baking sheets. Sprinkle with yellow cornmeal. Gash tops diagonally every 2-3 inches, about ⅛″ deep.

Beat one egg white, add 1 tablespoon water. Brush on loaves. Cover and let rise about 1 hour. Bake at 375° for 20 minutes. Brush again with egg white and water mixture. Bake 15-20 minutes longer. Remove from sheets and cool. **Yield: 2 loaves**

New Orleans Style Muffalettas

Submitted by Alison Salloum

The bread is supposedly named after the Sicilian baker who brought them to New Orleans. Muffalettas have been around since the turn of the century and are said to have been the favorite of President Eisenhower.

**provolone cheese
polish ham
genoa salami
bologna
olive salad with siclian olives
pickled cauliflower
radishes
pepper
white onions
celery
vinegar
garlic and oregano
round muffaletta
bread with sesame seeds
olive oil**

Place all ingredients on the   muffaletta bread and drizzle with olive oil. Cut into sections as desired. **Serves:** 2 or more

St. Expedite

Submitted by Mel Leavitt, Historian, Author and TV Commentator

This is the story of the Saint who never existed. Oh, he existed all right—in the hearts, the minds, and imaginations of thousands of Orleanians who believed in him when all else failed, for he expedited action in time of great peril. He was there, especially during the horrible years of plague that killed almost 100,000 in our city from yellow fever, malaria, cholera and typhoid. His name was St. Expedite...the expeditor. There was only one problem—search of church records revealed no record of such a person, much less a sanctified being.

St. Expedite—not real? Well, then who dreamed him up and why? Legend has it that it actually started in Paris. Some Parisian nuns received a box of relics from Rome for their new chapel. No clue to their identity could be found except the label on the outside. It read simply "E Spedito," followed by the date. The nuns did not read Italian, so they failed to realize E Spedito meant Sent Off. Instead, they assumed it was the name of the Saint whose relics they received. They therefore named their chapel for St. Expeditus...and a new cult was formed.

Eventually, the Saint's name became a kind of pun. St. Expeditus was the patron Saint of hustle, the expeditor, the guy who got things done.

French Bread (Pain Francais)

Submitted by Alley Frieze

2 cups	warm water
1 package (1 ounce)	dry yeast
3 Tablespoons	soft shortening
1 Tablespoon	salt
6 cups	sifted all-purpose flour
	corn meal
1	egg white
2 Tablespoons	water

Pour 1½ cups warm water into a large mixing bowl; sprinkle yeast in remaining ½ cup of warm water, stir until dissolved and add to water in large bowl. Add shortening, salt and 3 cups of the flour. Beat until smooth. Add remaining flour to form a stiff dough, working in with hands if necessary (and it is). Remove dough to floured board and knead until smooth and elastic (about 10 minutes). Place dough in greased bowl, turn over so all sides will be greased. Cover with clean, dry cloth, set in warm place free from drafts. The dough should double in bulk about 1½ to 2 hours. Punch down; let rise again until almost double in bulk again (this is important). Punch down again and divide dough into three parts. Shape with hands into three long loaves, tapering the ends. Place on greased cookie sheets that have been sprinkled lightly with corn meal. Make several gashes about ⅛-inch deep on each loaf. Do not cover; let rise about one hour or until double in bulk. Preheat oven to 400 degrees. For crisp crust, place shallow pan of water on bottom of oven. Beat egg whites slightly with water; brush loaves. Bake 20 minutes; brush again; bake 20 minutes longer until brown. Cool well. **Hint:** May be frozen to maintain freshness and reheated in foil. **Yield:** 3 loaves

Medaillons De Veau Aux Champignons

Submitted by Broussard's Restaurant

2 (3 ounces each)	veal medaillons, ¼-inch thick
	salt and pepper to taste
	flour
	clarified butter
3	champignon mushrooms
1	shallot, finely chopped
1 Tablespoon	brandy
2 ounces	demi glace
1 cup	whipping cream

Lightly season veal with salt and pepper. Turn lightly in flour, sauté for 5 minutes in clarified butter. Place medaillons on plate and keep warm.

Quarter three mushrooms and chopped shallot and put in sauté pan. Flambé with brandy, add demi glace and whipping cream. Reduce over medium heat until the mixture is smooth and creamy. Cover medaillons with sauce and serve. **Serves:** 2

Veal Piccata

Submitted by Goffredo Fraccaro, La Riviera Restaurant

12	veal scallops, 4-5 pounds total salt and pepper to taste flour
3 ounces	butter
2 Tablespoons	parsley, finely chopped juice of one lemon
2 Tablespoons	hot stock

Beat the scallops until thin and flat, but not broken. Sprinkle them with salt, pepper and flour.

Melt ⅔ of the butter in a wide pan. Add the veal. Turn up the heat and fry the veal quickly. Salt lightly.

When meat is done, place in heated serving dish and keep hot. Add the parsley, lemon juice and remaining butter and stock to the pan. Stir well and as soon as the sauce is bubbling, pour it over the veal. Serve immediately. **Serves:** 6

Annie Christmas "The First Lady of the Waterfront"

Submitted by Mel Leavitt, Historian, Author and TV Commentator

Down on the New Orleans wharves men still talk with awe and reverence of Annie Christmas. She was the First Lady of the Waterfront, nothin' like her. She stood six feet eight and weighed nearly 250 pounds. Naturally, she was very strong (but in a feminine sort of way).

Annie Christmas was rather sensitive about her size. She didn't want to make the boys feel selfconscious, being generally bigger and stronger than they were. So she wore a neat mustache and had the word "Mother" tattooed on her right forearm.

Annie was a bright beacon on the foggiest morning. Her powerful voice could be heard a mile away. The tough old buzzards who poled those flatboats and keelboats downriver feared no one except Annie Christmas.

"I was raised on alligators and weaned on panther's milk! Yahoo!" those varmints would scream and yell. They were noisy and mean and dirty and lusty and itchin' for a fight after three months on the river. But when they saw Annie standing there, nonchalantly pitching cotton, six or eight bales at a time, they became terrible quiet and awful sedate.

"Just where did Annie come from?" everybody wondered. She dressed like a man. She worked like a man. But she looked like a woman, smelled like a woman (all sweet and sexy). She could balance a barrel of flour on her head while carrying two more barrels, one under each arm. Once, she towed a keelboat to Natchez on a dead run and never lost her breath. Or so they say.

They also say that Annie could outdrink anybody in Orlins. She once put down a barrel of beer and "chased" it with ten quarts of rotgut whisky. She

134

chugged one, then the other, without so much as a pause. Not even a burp. (That would have been "unladylike.")

Every now and then, it's said, Annie would switch to her feminine persuasion. She bought perfume by the barrel and mascara by the vat. When Annie Christmas stepped out, she was 250 pounds of coal-black, seductive, enticing, female woman, you bet. She once rented a barge and filled it with the finest New Orleans "fancy women." She operated the first marine brothel on the Mississippi, catering to river rats and others longing for female companionship.

On dress-up occasions, Annie Christmas would promenade in red satin gowns and scarlet plumes, wearing her incredible thirty foot long necklace. It supposedly contained a bead for every leg, ear, eye, or nose she had gouged from a dishonest man.

Being a sensitive family woman, she resented slurs that she was "loose" or "fancy." Annie, it's said, had twelve sons, each seven feet tall, all born at the same time. They protected her from everything except that one man who showed up on the wharves stronger than she was. Annie acted like a schoolgirl. She fell in love with him. She bought her first pair of size 14 patent-leather pumps. She took to wearing lipstick and giggling.

Alas, her new true love thought she was silly, and much too big. So he ditched her for someone six foot three. Annie never saw that man again. The story goes: Annie Christmas went to bed and never got up again. She died, they say, of exasperation, desperation, and self-expiration. Just laid down and started crying and crying—and finally suffocated, or maybe drowned on her own huge salty tears. That's what they say.

Her funeral was something. Nothing seen like it before or since or in between. Annie's body was placed on a black coffin and driven to the docks in a mammoth black hearse. It was pulled by twelve black horses, six to a side. And six to a side, her twelve black sons marched on the river. There, they placed Annie Christmas' coffin on a black barge one black night.

LIke a Viking burial, they floated her down the Mississippi and out into the Gulf of Mexico. Annie Christmas vanished forever. No obituary. No burial plot, tombstone, or epitaph. No sons either. Her sons went off looking for the no-good man who jilted their mother, and are still out there looking now.

We don't know if anyone found that no-good man. But every time an unidentified body comes floating down the Mississippi, some longshoreman's sure to say, "Bet that's his body. Bet that's him. That sweettalkin' no-good dude that broke ole Annie's heart."

That's what they say.

Mother's Floating Island

Submitted by The Alcée-Hymel Family

½ cup	sugar
½ teaspoon	salt
1 Tablespoon	cornstarch
2 cups	milk
4	eggs, separated
1 teaspoon	vanilla
⅓ cup	sugar for egg whites

Mix together ½ cup sugar, salt and cornstarch in saucepan. Scald milk, then pour over sugar mixture slowly, stirring well. Add beaten egg yolks, blend thoroughly, then cook slowly until mixture thickens. Cool, add vanilla. Beat egg whites until stiff, gradually beating in ⅓ cup sugar, until peaks form. Gently fold whites into custard, being careful not to break up the stiffly beaten whites. They will float through the custard like little islands; that is why it is floating island. Chill and serve. **Serves: 4**

Chapter III

Living Legends

This chapter will be of special interest to people who have asked themselves, "How did crawfish get their name?", "Which side of a chicken is most tender?", and "What is the origin of the word 'barbecue'?" The answers and the recipes follow!

Barbecue

Submitted by Wildy Templet

The early settlers of Louisiana used smoke (boucan) to prepare and preserve most foods. French settlers of the colony are said to have observed this particular method of food preparation from the native Indians.

Legend has it that French explorer André Penicaut came upon a ritual feast where a group of Indians were roasting a large four-legged animal and remarked, "c'est-roti a un barbe et un queue," meaning "This roast has a beard and a tail!" Hence, we have "un barbe-et-un-que" or "barbecue."

Barbecued Spareribs

Submitted by Austin Leslie, Chez Helene Restaurant

2 sides (12 large ribs each side)	spareribs (cut in sections) salt and freshly ground pepper salad oil barbecue sauce (see below)

Place spareribs in large pot. Cover with boiling water. When water returns to boil, reduce heat and simmer for 30 minutes. Remove ribs from pot and place on baking pans. Salt and pepper ribs to taste, then oil ribs lightly and brown both sides under broiler. Place ribs flat in roasting pans and cover with barbecue sauce. Grill over hot coals until tender (or bake at 350° 1-1½ hours or until tender). Baste and turn ribs every 15 minutes. **Serves: 8**

Barbecue Sauce:

1 cup	onion, finely chopped
3 toes	garlic, finely chopped
1 stick	butter
2 cups	catsup
¼ cup	brown sugar
1 teaspoon	salt
½ teaspoon	pepper
½ teaspoon	Tabasco®
¼ cup	white vinegar
1 Tablespoon	chili powder
dash	Worcestershire sauce

Sauté onions and garlic in butter until tender. Add the remaining ingredients and simmer for 10 minutes.

liquid smoke
more Tabasco
horseradish (1 tlbs.)
Cajun Power Garlic Sauce
can tomato sauce

Grilled Shrimp with Tasso Pasta

Submitted by Flagons, a wine bar

24 large	shrimp, peeled and deveined
2 teaspoons	seafood seasoning
½ pound	tasso, cut in ¼-inch cubes
1 ounce	clarified butter
3 cups	heavy cream
24 ounces	fettucine noodles, cooked and drained
½ cup	mixture of parmesan and romano cheeses, grated

Seafood Seasoning:

2 teaspoons	black pepper
½ teaspoon	cayenne
1½ teaspoons	paprika
1½ teaspoons	granulated onion
2 teaspoons	granulated garlic
¾ teaspoon	thyme

Place shrimp on metal skewers, 6 shrimp per person. Sprinkle lightly with seasoning salt. Grill quickly over charcoal or gas turning once until shrimp are pink and firm to the touch (about 4 to 5 minutes). Remove from heat and place on an oven-proof platter in a warm oven.

Sauté tasso in the clarified butter over medium high heat until the cubes begin to crisp. Add cream and rest of seafood seasoning and cook until cream boils and begins to reduce. Add fettucine and toss. Add cheeses and toss until cheese is melted.

Divide pasta between four warm plates. Remove shrimp from skewers and arrange around pasta. Serve piping hot. **Serves:** 4

Grilled Salmon With Sauce Choron

Submitted by Chef Daniel Bonnot

4 portions (7 ounces each)	**fresh salmon (grilled approximately 5 minutes on each side)**

Hollandaise Sauce for Sauce Choron:

3	**egg yolks**
9 ounces	**melted butter**
2½ teaspoons	**lemon juice**
	salt and pepper to taste

Whip egg yolks, adding a touch of water to loosen the yolks, over a double boiler until cooked. Do not scramble. This should have a custard-like consistency. Remove from heat and slowly add melted butter. Add lemon juice and season with salt and pepper. Add bearnaise reductions.

Bearnaise Reduction:

3 Tablespoons	**minced shallots**
⅓ cup	**red wine vinegar**
5 fresh	**green peppercorns**
¼ cup	**tarragon**

Combine ingredients and heat over low flame until complete evaporation. Add this reduction to hollandaise sauce.

Add 1 tablespoon tomato paste to complete Sauce Choron. **Serves:** 4

The Legend of the Cocktail

Submitted by Ella Brennan, Commander's Palace Restaurant

New Orleans has been the city of civilized drinking for almost two centuries. Meeting and socializing over one of our famous frothy cocktails or a steamy café au lait is more than a tradition; it is a celebration of a way of life.

The American cocktail was, according to legend, born and named in New Orleans' Vieux Carré almost two hundred years ago. Folklore relates that in 1793, during the uprising of blacks in Santo Domingo, a young apothecary from a distinguished French family escaped to New Orleans, salvaging a secret family recipe for a liquid tonic compounded of bitters and brandy. The apothecary, Antoine Amadée Peychaud, soon opened a pharmacy at 437 Royal Street, where he dispensed his cure-all tonic over the counter to both the ailing and the thirsty. More to the point, Peychaud served his soothing spiced brandy in a unique way—pouring his potent potion into the larger side of a double-ended "egg cup," known in French as a coquetier, which through the mispronunciation became cock-tay, and finally cocktail. Soon all New Orleans was imbibing his brandy cocktail, which differed from the usual brandy toddy by the addition of bitters. Thus the cocktail was born.

Sazerac

Submitted by A.C. Doan

1 ounce	bourbon
3 drops	bitters
1 teaspoon	grenadine
1 teaspoon	Pernod
	lemon twist

Pour bourbon, bitters and grenadine into cocktail shaker and mix thoroughly with a cocktail spoon—do not shake. Add Pernod to a pre-chilled old fashioned glass. Thoroughly coat the inside of the glass with Pernod, tilting it every which way and then pouring off any excess. Strain mixture from cocktail shaker into chilled coated glass and top with a twist of lemon. **Hint:** When coating the glass with Pernod, add a little New Orleans flair to your drink preparation by twirling the glass in the air and catching it. **Yield:** 1 drink

Metairie Country Club Bloody Marys

Submitted by Betty Vega

8 ounces	lemon juice
18 ounces	vodka
8 ounces	Lea & Perrins® Worcestershire sauce
1 can (10 ounces)	bouillon soup
1 can (46 ounces)	V-8 Juice®
1 can (46 ounces)	tomato juice

Blend and serve chilled. **Yield:** 20 drinks

Brandy Coffee Cooler

Submitted by P.J.'s Coffee & Tea, Inc.

This drink can be served in place of dessert, or by itself as a refreshing afternoon or evening beverage.

1½ ounces	brandy
4 ounces	cold coffee (a full-bodied coffee should be used such as Sumatran, Costa Rican or French Roast)
1 ounce	cream
1 ounce	coffee liqueur
1 teaspoon	sugar
	crushed ice
	coffee ice cream

Shake brandy, coffee, cream, liqueur, sugar and ice together well. Strain into a 12-ounce glass. Add a scoop of ice cream. **Serves:** 1

How Hushpuppies
Got The Name

Submitted by Davelynn Burch

Long ago in the Antebellum days, cooks could always be found in the kitchen behind the plantation home, cooking up sumptuous feasts for the plantation owners and the workers. While the cooks were busy cooking, the hounds that lived on the plantation would be attracted to the kitchen by the aromas of the good food. There they would sit at the back door of the kitchen and bark and whine because of their hunger. The cooks, feeling sorry for the poor hounds, would mix a quick batter of cornmeal and water which they would fry. As they threw these cornmeal balls out the back door, they would shout "Hush puppies! Hush puppies!"

Cajun Hushpuppies

Submitted by Alley Frieze

1 cup	flour
2 cups	cornmeal
1 Tablespoon	baking powder
1½ teaspoons	salt
2	eggs
1 small can	cream style corn
½	sweet red pepper, diced small
3	jalapeño peppers, diced small
1	onion, minced
½ cup	buttermilk
½ teaspoon	baking soda
	fat for frying

Mix all ingredients except fat together to make a batter. Scoop from a spoon into hot fat until done. For more tang, add a few drops Tabasco®. **Yield: 25**

Why Alligators are a Steamboat Captain's Best Friends

Courtesy of Riverwalk

It began years ago, when alligators in the Mississippi River were as thick as mud. Since alligator shoes and the like are no longer rare sights, the animals are. However, at the time, a steamboat couldn't pass without getting scores of them tangled in the wheels.

One steamboat captain, known only as Captain Tom, always carried 1,000 bottles of liniment to throw over to the injured gators to soothe their wounds. In return, when Captain Tom's boat got grounded on a sandbar, it's said that all the alligators gathered under the stern and pushed his boat clear over the bar. Much later, when Captain Tom died, every alligator in the river daubed his left ear with black mud as a sign of mourning for their lost friend.

Gator

Courtesy of Riverwalk

Alligators were on the endangered species list until about a decade ago, but not anymore. The efforts to save them have been so successful that Louisiana was able to establish a hunting season for them in the fall. Most of the interest in hunting them centers on the value of their skins, but they're good to eat too.

In order to prepare a good Creole-style alligator dish, melt ½ cup of butter in a heavy skillet. For ten minutes, sauté 1½ diced bell peppers, 1⅓ cups chopped onions, and 2½ cups chopped celery. Remove these with a slotted spoon. Add ½ cup of flour and blend with butter. Put the seasonings back in the skillet and add about 2 large cans (28 ounces each) of canned tomatoes, a little salt, cayenne, and bay leaves, 2 tablespoons of brown sugar, 8 whole cloves, and some garlic if you like. Bring to a boil. Add 4 pounds of alligator and simmer at low heat for about an hour. Just before serving, add Tabasco® or Louisiana hot sauce, a little lemon juice, and about ⅔ cup of good, dry white wine. Serve over hot rice.

There are several kinds of meat on an alligator. The tail is like the white veal and may be sautéed. The legs are dark, like beef shank, and must be stewed. The body meat is between the two, something like pork. You may substitute pork for the alligator in this recipe.

How Crawfish Came to Be

Submitted by Davelynn Burch

Many, many decades ago when the Acadians were still living in Nova Scotia, they were very close to their friends, the lobsters. For years the Acadians and lobsters lived together happily. One day an Acadian fisherman named Jean-Paul told his especially good friend the Lobster-King that the Acadians had been expelled from Nova Scotia because they refused to bow to the British Crown. The Lobster-King went into the ocean and told the other lobsters the sad news. The lobsters decided they could not bear to be parted from their friends, the Acadians, so when the time came for the Acadians to leave, the lobsters would leave also and follow the Acadians to a new home. The journey was long and hard for both. Many perished along the slow trek to the South. Because of all the hardships they suffered during the journey, the lobsters lost weight and began to decrease in size. By the time they reached the beautifully serene swamplands of Louisiana where they decided to stay, the lobsters were barely 6 inches long and weighed a few ounces. The Acadians and lobsters settled in the swamp and bayou areas of Louisiana happily. Today the Acadians are known as Cajuns and because the lobsters crawled all the way from Nova Scotia to be with their friends, they are known as Crawfish.

La Terrine D'Ecrevisses Au Coulis De Tomate (Crawfish Aspic with Fresh Tomato Sauce)

Submitted by Chef Michel Marcais, from La Fête 1984

18 ounces	crawfish tails, cooked and cleaned
1 bunch	parsley, chopped
4	ripe tomatoes, peeled and seeded
3 cups	clear fish aspic
3 teaspoons	olive oil
2 teaspoons	vinegar
1 pinch	fresh basil
	salt and pepper to taste

Mix crawfish tails, parsley, two chopped tomatoes with fish aspic. Mold in a rectangular dish.

Refrigerate until firm. Cut into 6 slices.

In blender, blend 2 tomatoes, olive oil, vinegar, and basil. Add salt and pepper to taste.

Serve sauce on side of crawfish aspic. **Serves:** 6

Crawfish Angel Hair Andrea

Submitted by Andrea's Restaurant

Crawfish:

4 pounds	whole crawfish to make 1 pound of crawfish meat
1 pound	crawfish tails to be used as garnish

Crawfish Sauté:

	crawfish meat from above
½ stick	butter
3 stalks	celery, chopped, Brunoise
1 medium	onion, chopped, Brunoise
1 medium	red bell pepper, chopped Brunoise
1	green bell pepper, chopped, Brunoise
½ teaspoon	chopped garlic
1 ounce	brandy
2 ounces	fresh dill (1 ounce chopped very fine, save 1 ounce for garnish)

Sauce:

	oil
	crawfish shells from above
2 stalks	celery, chopped
1 medium	onion, chopped
2	carrots, chopped
1	leek, chopped
2 cloves	garlic
1 Tablespoon	tomato paste
1 ounce	brandy
4 ounces	white wine
3 ounces	flour

2 quarts	fish stock
½ teaspoon	cayenne pepper
2	bay leaves
½ teaspoon	thyme
½ teaspoon	Lea & Perrins®
4 ounces	whipping cream
1½ pounds	angel hair pasta

Crawfish: Peel and boil 4 pounds of crawfish and save on a plate.

Sauce: Heat a pot on the stove and add a little oil. Add the crawfish shells, chopped vegetables and mix well. Then add two cloves of garlic, chopped, as well as the tomato paste. When everything is hot, add the brandy and flame. Add the white wine and let evaporate. Sprinkle the flour and mix well with a wire whisk and add the fish stock. Bring to a boil and let simmer for one hour and a half. Add the cayenne, bay leaves, thyme, salt and pepper to taste.

Crawfish Sauté: In a different pot add the butter and make hot. Add the celery, onion, red pepper, green pepper. Sauté very well and add the crawfish meat, stirring all the time. Add ½ teaspoon chopped garlic. When hot, flame with brandy and add the chopped dill.

Combine sauce and crawfish sauté as follows: When the sauce is ready, strain through a fine colander and add to the crawfish sauté with Lea & Perrins, salt and pepper to taste. If more taste is wished, add a little more cayenne. Do not make too spicy. Bring once again to a boil and add the cream.

Angel Hair Pasta: In a pot bring water to a boil with a light touch of salt and one tablespoon of olive oil. Add the angel hair and cook for 2 to 3 minutes or until they are al dente. Strain through colander and mix with the sauce. Garnish crawfish tails and fresh dill on top. **Serves: 8**

How Crawfish Came to New Orleans

Submitted by Michelle St. Romain

A long time ago, a group of Maine lobsters became sick and tired of the dreary weather and cold water of New England. They discussed their problem at length and decided they should find a new home. One morning they set out for the South. They decided they would keep swimming until they all agreed on a location. When they reached New York one lobster wanted to stay and become a Broadway star. The other lobsters thought she was crazy and they moved on. They had similar problems in Washington with Senator Lobster and in Hilton Head with Golfer lobster. A few lobsters retired in Miami. The most persistent continued to the gulf where they finally reached the shores of Louisiana. After their long journey, they had all shrunk because of the strenuous long distance swimming. These small lobsters were fruitful and multiplied. Very soon, Louisiana was crawling with the creatures, hence crawfish. The crawfish loved their beautiful new home in Louisiana and have lived there happily every after.

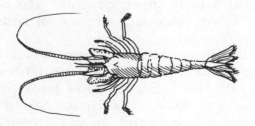

Crawfish Étouffée

Submitted by Austin Leslie, Chez Helene Restaurant

6 Tablespoons	brown roux
2 medium	onions, chopped
2 ribs	celery, chopped
1	green pepper, chopped
3 toes	garlic, chopped
3 cups	fish stock (hot)
1 cup	tomato purée
1 Tablespoon	lemon juice
½ teaspoon	cayenne pepper
¼ teaspoon	thyme
1 Tablespoon	Lea and Perrins® sauce
3 pounds	crawfish tails
1 cup	crawfish fat
½ cup	parsley, finely chopped
½ cup	green onions, finely chopped
½ cup	dry sherry (optional) salt and pepper to taste

Warm roux over low heat for 3 minutes. Add onions, celery, bell pepper, garlic and sauté slowly for 5 minutes. Then, slowly whisk in the hot fish stock and bring to a boil. When sauce reaches a boil, reduce heat to a simmer and add tomato purée, lemon juice, cayenne, thyme and Lea and Perrins sauce. Simmer uncovered for ½ hour, then strain sauce into another pot. Add crawfish tails and crawfish fat to pot and simmer covered for 15 minutes. Stir in chopped parsley, green onions, sherry and salt and pepper to taste. Serve over steamed rice. **Note:** Crawfish fat is picked from the head of the crawfish. It can be purchased, frozen, in New Orleans. **Serves:** 6

The Breaux Bridge Crawfish Festival

Courtesy of Calvin Trillin from American Fried
published by Doubleday. Copyright (c) 1972

The question in my mind when my wife Alice and I arrived at the Breaux Bridge Crawfish Festival was whether to enter the official crawfish-eating contest or content myself with acts of free-lance gluttony.

The world record at crawfish eating—the record, at least, according to Breaux Bridge, which is, by resolution of the Louisiana Legislature, the Crawfish Capital of the World—was set by a local man named Andrew Thevenet, who at one Crawfish Festival ate the tails of thirty-three pounds of crawfish in two hours. My doubts about being able to peel that much crawfish in two hours—not to speak of eating it—were increased by some stories I heard about tricks contestants have used in the past. One man was said to have perfected a method of peeling a crawfish with one hand and popping it into his mouth while reaching for the next crawfish with his other hand. Somebody told me that one contestant had spent the evening before the contest "lining his stomach with red beans and rice"—although that sounds to me at least contradictory and maybe suicidal. A pharmacy student who triumphed at the Crawfish Festival two years before I arrived in Breaux Bridge (festivals are held only every other year) drank orange juice with his crawfish instead of the traditional beer, and a friend had heard that the orange juice was laced with exotic chemicals (known only to people like pharmacy students) that somehow provided the same service for crawfish in the stomach that an electric trash-compactor provides for trash. In fairness, I should add that a former contestant from Lafayette told me the pharmacy student had used no tricks at all and was just a hungry boy.

Crawfish Versailles

Submitted by Gunter Preuss, The Versailles Restaurant

2 Tablespoons	sliced green onions
2 Tablespoons	minced garlic
1 Tablespoon	minced dry shallots
2 Tablespoons	fresh butter
½ cup	white wine
	juice of ¼ lemon
1¾ cups	medium bechamel sauce
1½ Tablespoons	fresh dill (1 Tablespoon dried)
1½ pounds	fresh boiled crawfish tails
	salt to taste
pinch	cayenne pepper
	parmesan cheese

Sauté onions, garlic and shallots in butter for 2 minutes without browning. Add white wine and lemon juice, reduce by ½. Add bechamel sauce and dill and recduce by another ⅓. Add crawfish tails and simmer 10 minutes. Salt to taste and add a pinch of cayenne pepper.

To serve: put in ramekins or small sea shells, sprinkle with freshly grated parmesan cheese and bake in 350° oven until cheese is golden. Garnish with boiled crawfish and serve. **Serves:** 6

Sauté of Fresh Louisiana Crawfish

Submitted by Commander's Palace Restaurant

This sauté of fresh Louisiana crawfish is a simple but spectacular dish—ideal for elegant entertaining. It is quick to assemble—all ingredients can be organized ahead—and the final preparation takes a mere 2 minutes.

Make sure not to overcook the crawfish; they are more delicate than shrimp, so you must be more careful.

Crawfish Rice:

½ stick	(4 Tablespoons) unsalted butter
1 medium	onion, finely chopped
2 stalks	celery, finely chopped
1	green bell pepper, finely choped
½ pound	cooked crawfish tails, peeled, deveined and chopped
1 cup	raw rice
1⅔ cups	crawfish or fish stock, heated
1 teaspoon	salt or to taste
2 sticks plus 2 Tablespoons (10 ounces)	unsalted butter, softened
1 pound	cooked crawfish tails, peeled and deveined
1 cup	chopped green onions
1 Tablespoon	Creole Seafood Seasoning®
1 Tablespoon	Worcestershire sauce

To make the rice: Melt butter in a saucepan over low heat. Add onion, celery, green bell pepper, and crawfish and sauté for 2 minutes. Add rice and mix well to coat rice with butter. Add boiling stock and salt, bring liquid back to a boil, cover pot tightly, and simmer until rice is tender and all the liquid has been absorbed, about 20 minutes. Set aside and keep warm.

In a frying pan melt 2 tablespoons butter and sauté crawfish tails and green onions with seafood seasoning and Worcestershire sauce until hot, stirring constantly. Remove from heat. Add the remaining softened butter, a piece at a time, tossing mixture gently until butter is incorporated in the sauce and sauce is creamy.

Serve immediately with crawfish rice and French bread.

Note: One pound live crawfish yields ½ pound peeled, cooked tails. **Serves:** 4

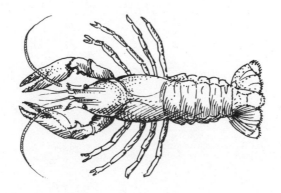

Patios

Submitted by Mildred L. Covert and Sylvia P. Gerson

New Orleans' picturesque patios, predominantly located in the Vieux Carré, are frequented in most tours of the city. The Creoles considered it a breach of etiquette to enter a home through the front door. They entered on the side by means of a patio or courtyard. One passes through a porte cochère, a wide gate, high enough to allow a coachman wearing his high hat to remain seated on the carriage. Patio is the Spanish equivalent of courtyard; in French it comes from the phrase coeur de maison, meaning "heart of the house."

Folklore relates an interesting interpretation of the origin of the word "patio." As the horsedrawn carriages pulled into the opened gates, the hoofbeats gradually slowed to a "pat-a-pat-pat," and the cry of "whoa, whoa" was heard until the carriage came to a stop. In imitation of the two sounds, the combination "pat-pat" and "whoa" soon became slurred, and the word "patio" emerged.

Creole Rice Custard
(Riz au Lait)

Submitted by The Alcée-Hymel Family

½ cup	washed rice
2 cups	water
1 cup	milk
handful	of currants or raisins
	sugar to taste
1	egg yolk
1 teaspoon	milk
	vanilla to taste

Boil rice in water until very tender and creamy. Add one cup of milk and currants or raisins and sugar. Let cook slowly for 15 minutes and remove from fire. Beat the yolk of an egg in a spoonful of milk, and stir in the rice. Add vanilla. Serve cold. **Serves:** 4

Shrimp Creole

Submitted by Aurrora Correia

½ cup	onion
½ cup	chopped celery
1 clove	garlic
3 Tablespoons	salad oil
1 can (1 pound)	tomatoes
1 can (8 ounces)	tomato sauce
2 teaspoons	salt
1 teaspoon	sugar
½ teaspoon	chili powder
1 Tablespoon	Lea & Perrins® Sauce
dash	Tabasco® sauce
1 teaspoon	cornstarch
2 teaspoons	water
1 pound	cleaned raw shrimp
½ cup	chopped green pepper

Sauté onion, celery and garlic in oil until tender. Combine tomatoes and tomato sauce with seasonings. Add to cooked vegetables. Cook on low fire for 45 minutes. Mix cornstarch with water, then stir into sauce. Cook until sauce thickens. Add shrimp and green pepper. Cover and cook on low fire until shrimp is done.

Hint: To make a thicker sauce, add more cornstarch. To make a thinner sauce, add more water. **Serves:** 4

An "Okay" Legend (Maybe)

Submitted by Robert K. McKay, WEZB/B-97 FM

When the Spanish Conquistadores first anchored their tall ships out in the gulf of Mexico and paddled their way up through the mouth of what we now know as the Mississippi River, they were greeted by a band of hospitable natives living along the turbulent river's bank.

This tribe of American Aborigines led by their Chief, Okeakuk, helped the explorers chart vast stretches of wilderness territory west of the big bend in the muddy waterway. They and their ancestors had hunted and fished this region for untold centuries. Okeakuk's braves protected their visitors from hostile neighboring tribes and he commanded his women to attend to the soldiers' every need.

So accomodating was this predecessor of Louisiana's first European and African citizens, that his name even to this day remains synonymous with hospitality and a sense of well being. He was truly "Okay."

Wild Ducks with Olives

Submitted by Leon Irwin, Jr., King of Rex, 1954

1	duck (3-4 pounds)
1 medium	onion
1 Tablespoon	lard (shortening)
1 Tablespoon	olive oil
2 teaspoons	flour
	boiling water
1 cup	green olives
	salt and pepper

Salt and pepper duck well. Tie feet and wings down. Peel medium onion and put it inside duck.

In a large iron pot put a level tablespoon of lard (shortening) and a tablespoon of olive oil. When fat is hot, brown duck without putting top of pot on. The duck must be well browned all over. Take duck out. Add flour, smoothing until brown. Gradually add boiling water until it is about one inch deep in pot. Put duck back in pot and cover—but not entirely. Steam must escape.

Smother this for about two hours over medium fire. After 1½ hours of cooking time add a cup of sliced green olives. Season with salt and pepper to taste. **Hint:** When ready to serve, you may add some red wine if you like. Be careful not to use too much salt because the olives are salty. **Serves:** 4-6

Trout Pecan

Submitted by Kenita Grabiak, Brennan's Restaurant

10 ounces	**fillet of speckled trout**
	flour
10 Tablespoons	**butter**
1 Tablespoon	**Lea & Perrins Worcestershire Sauce®**
½ cup	**coarsely chopped pecans**
¾ cup	**lemon butter sauce**

Dust fish lightly in flour and let butter simmer in sauce pan. Sauté fish on both sides. After it is completely cooked, remove fish and allow butter to slightly brown. When butter is browned, skim off excess grease. Allow remaining butter and drippings to cool in pan for about 10 minutes. Then stir in the Lea & Perrins, pecans and the lemon butter sauce and remove from the fire immediatcly. Spoon over hot trout. (It may be necessary to reheat fish.) **Serves: 1**

Anecdote

Submitted by Chef Daniel Bonnot

If you are a true chicken gourmet, you know the right side is the most tender because a chicken always stands on his left leg!

Austin's Fried Chicken

Submitted by Austin Leslie, Chez Helene Restaurant

1½ cups	peanut oil for frying
1 (3 to 3½ pounds)	fryer, cut up
	salt and pepper
1	egg, lightly beaten
1 cup	light cream or Half and Half
1 cup	water
½ cup	all purpose flour

Preheat oil in frying pan to about 350°. Wash chicken pieces under cold water and pat dry. Sprinkle with salt and pepper. Make egg batter by combining egg, cream, water, salt and pepper. Dip pieces of chicken first in egg batter to coat and then in flour. Add chicken pieces to skillet, meatiest parts first. Do not crowd. Turn to brown on all sides. If oil pops, reduce flame. Cook until meat is tender and skin crisp, about 10 to 12 minutes. **Serves:** 4

Chicken Spaghetti

Submitted by Mercedes Andrus

In this recipe, the sauce and spaghetti are mixed together, instead of being served separately. A real winner!

1 (5-6 pounds)	**hen**
2 large	**onions, chopped**
2 large	**bell peppers, chopped**
2 cloves	**garlic, minced**
5 ribs	**celery, chopped**
¼ cup	**olive oil**
1 can (1 pound)	**whole tomatoes**
2 cans (6 ounces each)	**Italian tomato paste**
	reserved chicken stock
	salt, black pepper, poultry seasoning to taste
1 cup	**grated romano cheese**
1 can (6 ounces)	**mushrooms**
1 pound	**spaghetti**

Boil hen, remove from bone and reserve stock. Sauté onions, bell pepper, garlic, and celery in olive oil. Add tomatoes, tomato paste, and 1 quart chicken stock. Add salt, pepper, 1 teaspoon poultry seasoning. Allow to cook slowly for 3 hours, adding stock if necessary. Add ½ cup romano cheese during the last ½ hour of cooking, together with mushrooms and cooked chicken. Boil spaghetti for 12 minutes. Rinse in cold water. Add sauce and chicken to spaghetti and allow to stand 1-2 hours before serving. Offer additional cheese while serving. Sauce with chicken can be frozen. **Serves:** 6

Fried Rice and Chicken

Submitted by Mercedes Andrus (Judge Alexander Andrus)

2 large	fryers (3-4 pounds each)
6 ounces	olive oil
2	onions, chopped
1	bell pepper, chopped
6 stems	celery, chopped
1 bottle (2 ounces)	capers
1 can (1 pound)	whole peeled tomatoes
1 box (2 ounces)	raisins
½ cup	dry vermouth
1 bottle (6 ounces)	olives stuffed with pimento
3 cups	raw rice
3 cups	boiling water
	salt, red and black pepper
	poultry seasoning

Cut fryers into pieces and brown well in olive oil in large black pot. Remove chicken and add about ⅔ of the chopped vegetables and additional oil. Cook until wilted. Add capers, tomatoes (crushed whole tomatoes), raisins, vermouth and then place chicken pieces into pot so as to immerse pieces. Cook on medium low heat until chicken is tender (about 45 to 60 minutes). Remove from heat and remove chicken from pot. When chicken is cool remove meat from bone and chop into bite-size pieces. Chop skin into very fine pieces and add chopped chicken and skin to liquid, together with olives which have been sliced into thin strips.

In separate large pot cook remaining vegetables in oil until wilted. Increase heat to very hot and add raw rice stirring constantly until grains turn milky white (do not burn). Then add boiling water and stir vigorously until evaporating water level meets top of settled rice. Reduce heat to low, cover pot and let cook for 1 hour (do not peek, this lets steam escape). At end of hour remove top and gently stir rice (do not disturb gratin) to remove any excess moisture and let rice dry out. Stir rice gently into chicken and sauce and season with salt, red pepper and poultry seasoning to taste. Reheat before serving. **Serves:** 8

Chicken Stew

Submitted by the Bergeron Family

½ cup	cooking oil
½ cup	flour
1	hen, 4-5 pounds
1 large	onion, chopped
5 or 6 cloves	garlic, minced
½	sweet pepper, chopped
2 ribs	celery, chopped
	boiling water

Heat oil in heavy aluminum pot. Add flour and cook on medium heat, stirring constantly until dark brown. Cut chicken into serving pieces and add to mixture. Cook for about 15 minutes. Add remaining ingredients and sauté well. Add several cups of boiling water and simmer until chicken is tender. **Serves:** 6

Chapter IV

Food Legends

It's no coincidence that certain foods have been "invented" in New Orleans. Red beans and rice, for instance, became a staple meal for Mondays when the wash was done. This chapter has many interesting stories about food and some variations of the recipes created from those stories.

Louisiana Red Hot

Courtesy of Riverwalk

Christopher Columbus headed west seeking the riches and spices of the mysterious East, including black pepper. Finding not a grain of it in the New World that he accidentally discovered, he took back red pepper and introduced it to Europe.

Capiscum, the scientific term for edible peppers, and Cajuns seem to go together, and in fact, some of the most savory and potent pepper sauces made anywhere come from southern Louisiana and especially from Iberia Parish.

The most famous of all Iberia pepper sauces is Tabasco®, which is made on Avery Island, the magnificent bird sanctuary and gardens near the town of New Iberia. Edmund McIlhenny, a lover of well-seasoned food, began experimenting with condiments made from fine red peppers grown on his plantation from seeds brought back about 1853 from Mexico by an American veteran of the Mexican War.

After the Civil War, McIlhenny became good friends with General Hazzard, Union administrator for southern Louisiana. It so happened that the general's father was E. C. Hazzard of New York City, head of the largest wholesale grocery house in the country. After the son sent his father a sample of McIlhenny's pepper sauce, the old man insisted on introducing it commercially. The rest is history.

Pickled Peppers

Submitted by Merritt Robertson

This recipe was given to James H. Robertson by a drilling contracter (oil well), Mose Browning, and Mrs. Robertson has been using it for years and has never lost a pepper. She uses jalapeño and yellow wax or banana and bell peppers. She also uses gallon jugs to can in, mixing the peppers to get the right hot taste.

	peppers of choice (leave stems on)
1 teaspoon	plain salt per quart white vinegar
½-1 teaspoon	turmeric

Wash peppers, leaving stems on them and pack them tightly in jars. Add 1 teaspoon plain salt per quart and cover with white vinegar. Place jars in cold water in a pan that will bring water to within an inch of the top of the jars, place lids on top of jars, not sealing; bring water to boil. Remove jars from water and drain vinegar off. Sprinkle ½ to 1 teaspoon of turmeric on top of peppers. Cover with cold vinegar and seal. Peppers will be ready to eat in 3 to 4 days. **Variation:** For Hot Party Pak, use same recipe as above, adding carrots, celery and cauliflower to peppers. Each vegetable will retain its own taste.

Marinade Sauce

Submitted by Abe Ritman, Abe's Sea & Sirloin Restaurant

This sauce can be used for crab claws, crabmeat, salads and for meat and fish to be cooked later.

2 bundles	scallions (green onions)
14	individual onions
1 large stalk	celery, 14 individual stems
1 large bunch	parsley
	all the fresh garlic you can stand or like
	juice of 6 lemons
1 heaping Tablespoon	salt
1 heaping Tablespoon	black pepper
1 bottle (5 ounces)	Lea & Perrins® Worcestershire Sauce
3 pints	salad oil

Clean onions (using tops and bottoms), the celery, and remove as many heavy stems from the parsley as you can.

Slice the onions, celery and parsley in 1-inch pieces and chop in food chopper. Add the garlic. Do not blend. This should produce about ½ gallon of chopped vegetables. Add the rest of the ingredients and allow to sit over night.

This marinade does not have to be refrigerated, except when marinating raw meat or fish (refrigerate for 8 to 10 hours). Crabmeat, crab claws, tomatoes, onions or other fresh items need only to be marinated for ½ hour.

You can use your imagination by adding other spices or flavors that you might like: pickle juice, parmesan cheese or an herb or low calorie dressing. **Hint:** Garlic powder or lemon concentrate may be substituted for the real thing.

Horseradish Sauce

Submitted by Gerald L. Andrus, King of Rex, 1960

1 teaspoon	prepared mustard
2 Tablespoons	prepared horseradish vinegar dash of onion juice and Tabasco®
1 Tablespoon	tarragon salt and pepper to taste
½ pint	cream

Mix mustard and horseradish. Blend in vinegar one teaspoon at a time until mixture is smooth. Add onion juice, Tabasco, tarragon, salt and pepper and then cream. Serve over brisket or baked fish.
Yield: 1 cup sauce

Spicy Barbecue Shrimp

Submitted by Lynn B. Stropolo

4 pounds	jumbo shrimp with heads
4 sticks	butter or margarine
1 Tablespoon	Tabasco® sauce
6 cloves	garlic, crushed
2 Tablespoons	Lea & Perrins® Worcestershire Sauce
1 Tablespoon	cayenne pepper
½ ounce	black pepper
⅛ cup	lemon juice

Soak shrimp for 10 minutes in salt water before cooking. Melt butter and add the rest of the ingredients. Drain shrimp and lay in shallow pan and pour sauce over them. Bake for 45 minutes at 350°.
Serves: 8

Food For Medicinal Purposes

Courtesy of Riverwalk

"Got a rash?" Apply crushed crab and crawfish eyes. Apply banana leaves to your forehead for headaches, and plantation leaves for open sores. Take oak leaf tea for diarrhea. If you have lockjaw, drink roach tea, which is guaranteed to get you talking again, but you may develop the urge to crawl on the floor.

Mushrooms Stuffed With Crabmeat

Submitted by La Provence Restaurant

1	red bell pepper, diced
1	green bell pepper, diced
1 bunch	green onions, diced
½ bunch	parsley, diced
1 stick	butter
1 pound	mushrooms, diced
½ quart	cream
1 pound	fresh crabmeat
1 cup	bread crumbs
1 cup	swiss and parmesan cheese, grated and mixed
	salt and cayenne pepper to taste
1 dozen	large mushrooms

173

Sauce:

3	green onions or 2 large french shallots, diced
¼ stick	butter
1 can (12-16 ounces)	tomato sauce
3 ounces	cognac
1 cup	cream
	salt and cayenne pepper to taste

Sauté peppers, onion and parsley with ½ stick of the butter, until transparent. Meanwhile sauté the diced mushrooms with the other ½ stick of butter until almost done. Add to the vegetables. Add the cream and cook about 5 minutes. Add crabmeat. Just heat the crabmeat and remove from heat. Add bread crumbs and cheeses, until the mixture is firm. Add more bread crumbs slowly if necessary. Season to taste with the salt and pepper. Let cool and form into balls. Take the large mushrooms and cut a flat on the crown, so that it will stand up straight. Take stuffing and place on the stem. Cook in a 450° oven for 10-15 minutes or until golden brown.

For sauce: Sauté onions in butter, add tomato sauce and cook for about 5 minutes stirring frequently. When the liquid has reduced, add cognac. Reduce the liquid again. Add cream and cook until the sauce has a smooth consistency. Season with salt and pepper to taste. Spoon sauce onto the plate and place heated mushrooms on plate and serve. **Yield:** 12 mushrooms

Crab Stew

Submitted by Marilyn E. Barthe

4 pounds	raw crabs
3 Tablespoons	flour
4 Tablespoons	cooking oil
2 medium	onions, chopped
5 cloves	garlic, minced
2 cups	tomato sauce
4 cups	water
¼ cup	parsley
2 sprigs	thyme
1 teaspoon	margarine
	salt and pepper to taste
¼ teaspoon	liquid crab boil

Steam crabs until pink, then drain. Brown flour in cooking oil, then sauté onions and garlic until tender. Add tomato sauce and let cook for 10 minutes on low fire. Add water, parsley, thyme, margarine, salt, pepper and liquid crab boil to taste. Simmer on a low fire until cooked. **Serves:** 4-6

Black-eyed Peas on New Year's

Courtesy of Riverwalk

For more than a century, the New Year's tradition of eating black-eyed peas has been observed in Louisiana. There are countless tales attempting to explain how this tradition got started. One thing ties them all together. The small cream-colored pea, actually a bean, with the "black eye" in the center is supposed to bring good luck.

One story tells of how a poor farmer who ate black-eyed peas on New Year's Day, started working on his fence. While digging a posthole, thinking gloomy thoughts of the coming year's mortgage and crop problems, he unearthed a pot of Spanish gold doubloons that had been buried there during the colonial period, before Louisiana became part of the United States.

Folklore promises that a person will earn a dollar for every pea that he eats on New Year's. Even at this rate, however, most persons would make only a few thousand dollars at best during the coming year. Of course, when this tale was first started, an income in the thousands would have been a considerable salary. Perhaps, now we should all believe that each pea is worth ten dollars!

An ancillary belief is that the eating of cabbage or other greens on New Year's will bring money.

Black-eyed Peas

Submitted by Austin Leslie, Chez Helene Restaurant

1 pound	black-eyed peas
2 medium	onions, diced
1 rib	celery, finely chopped
2 toes	garlic, finely chopped
4 sprigs	parsley, chopped
1 pound	pickled pork rib tips or smoked shoulder of ham, cubed or smoked ham hocks salt and pepper to taste
4 cups	cooked rice

Pick over peas before cleaning and remove any bruised or spotted ones. Soak in water overnight in a covered pot. Add diced onion to peas while they are soaking. The following day, strain and pour off water. Return peas and onions to pot. Add celery, garlic, parsley and pickled meat. Fill pot with water just to cover ingredients. Cook over a medium flame and simmer for 2½ to 3 hours. Add salt and pepper to taste. Serve over boiled rice. **Serves:** 4

Smothered Cabbage

Submitted by Austin Leslie, Chez Helene Restaurant

1 large or 2 small	heads of cabbage (quartered and cored)
3 Tablespoons	bacon dripping or vegetable oil
2	onions, chopped
4 toes	garlic, finely chopped
½ pound	pickled rib tips, diced
½ pound	seasoning ham, diced
1 teaspoon	salt
½ teaspoon	white pepper
¼ teaspoon	red pepper flakes

Soak cabbage in water. Shake off excess water and place in pot with heated bacon drippings or vegetable oil. Add remaining ingredients and simmer for 45 minutes. Stir occasionally. **Serves:** 4

The Molasses Flood

Courtesy of Riverwalk

New Orleans' old water-supply system, built before the Civil War, had a 90,000 square foot reservoir in the Uptown part of the city. When the present waterworks were built in 1909, the tank was emptied and rented to the Sugar Planters Storage and Distributing Company for keeping blackstrap molasses, the largest such storage facility in the world at the time.

Ten days after the tank was filled, the walls burst with a roar and 600,000 gallons of blackstrap oozed into the nearby streets. The sweet tide picked up two 15-ton boilers on one street and left a 7-foot high tidemark on a brick wall opposite the reservoir. For blocks around, the people rushed to the scene with cans, pots, and tubs and filled them with molasses. The streetcars splashed through the thick flood and streaked themselves with sweet-smelling color. Barefoot children waded in the molasses-filled gutters.

The streets had to be flooded with three million gallons of water to carry the diluted blackstrap back-of-town, toward the outlying swamps. New Orleans for days was a sticky-sweet place. Predictions of a massive invasion by ants and other insects proved to be only too correct. What a sweet time it was!

Camellia Grill's Pecan Pie

Submitted by Michael Shwartz, Camellia Grill

The pecan could be called the "state nut" of Louisiana and the pecan pie at Camellia Grill has become world famous during the decades since its introduction. It is loaded with pecans, while the filling is firm, moist, with just the right sweetness. Many people come to Camellia Grill just to eat this dessert.

4	eggs
¼ teaspoon	salt
¼ cup	melted butter
1¼ cups	light corn syrup
1¼ cups	firmly packed brown sugar
1 teaspoon	vanilla extract
1	unbaked 9-inch pastry shell
1 cup	chopped pecans

Beat eggs with a wire whisk or fork. Add salt, butter, corn syrup, sugar, and vanilla; mix well. Pour into pastry shell; sprinkle with pecans. Bake at 350° for 45-50 minutes.

Hint: Pecan pie is a very delicate pie to make. The baking directions must be followed exactly, in order to avoid burning the pecans on top of the pie, and to have the filling come out right.

Serves: 6-8

Sbisa's Chocolate Sin Cake

Submitted by Café Sbisa

10 ounces	semisweet chocolate
10 ounces	unsalted butter
	(room temperature)
1½ cups	sugar
8 large	eggs

Butter a 9-inch × 1½-inch round cake pan liberally. Line the bottom with waxed paper and butter the paper. Preheat oven to 350°.

In the top of a double boiler, melt the chocolate over hot water. Add the butter and stir until the butter has melted and the mixture is smooth.

Remove from heat. Whisk the sugar gradually into the chocolate mixture until mixture is thick. In a separate bowl, beat the eggs until they are foamy. Then stir them into the chocolate mixture until they are well incorporated.

Pour the mixture into the prepared pan and place the pan in a 14-inch × 11-inch baking pan. Add enough boiling water to come halfway up the sides of the baking pan. Bake in the center of oven for 1½ hours.

Remove the cake pan and let set for 10 minutes. Invert onto a flat plate. Chill, then serve at room temperature with coffee whipped cream.

Coffee Whipped Cream:

1 cup	heavy cream
2 Tablespoons	powdered sugar
1 Tablespoon	strong coffee

Beat the heavy cream until it just begins to hold shape. Sift powdered sugar over the top and beat until cream holds soft peaks. Stir in coffee. Spoon some onto each serving of cake. **Yield:** 1 cake

Sbisa's Pecan Pie

Submitted by Café Sbisa

5 ounces	butter
1 ounce	Meyer's rum
1 cup	dark brown sugar
¼ cup	flour
4	eggs
1½ cups	Karo® dark corn syrup
	pinch salt
2	unbaked 9-inch pie shells
3 cups	pecans

Melt butter and combine with rum, brown sugar, flour, eggs, corn syrup and salt. Beat until smooth and thoroughly mixed. Fill pie shells level full with pecans. Pour batter over pecans to rim of pie shells. Bake at 325° for 45 minutes. Cool. Serve with whipped cream. **Yield:** 2 pies

Pecan Pie

Submitted by Mary Michael

1 cup	white corn syrup
1 cup	dark brown sugar
⅓ teaspoon	salt
⅓ cup	melted butter
1 teaspoon	vanilla
3	eggs (slightly beaten)
1	unbaked 9-inch pie shell
1 heaping cup	shelled pecans

Combine syrup, sugar, salt, butter, vanilla and mix well. Add slightly beaten eggs. Pour into unbaked pie shell. Sprinkle pecans over all. Bake in 350° oven for 45 minutes. When cool, you may top with whipped cream or ice cream. . .but nothing tops this! **Yield:** 1 pie

The Legend of the Roman Candy Man

Submitted by Victoria Salloum

The Roman Candy Man has been driving his red and white wagon through the streets of New Orleans since 1915. The business was started by the grandfather of the present Roman Candy Man, Sam Conese. He was a fruit vendor who also sold stone, coal and firewood. One day he decided to sell the candy his mother made. He was afraid to call it Italian candy, fearing that only Italians would buy it. Instead, he called it Roman chewing candy. Conese kept several mules and travelled all over, sometimes taking the ferry to the west bank. After it became impractical to keep a stable, he limited himself to one mule and reduced his route.

Today, when people hear the familiar clip-clip and gong, they still come and buy Roman candy.

Terri's Old Fashioned Taffy (Chewing Candy)

Submitted by Terri Aimée

2 cups	sugar
½ cup	corn syrup
¼ teaspoon	cream of tartar
½ cup	water
1 teaspoon	vanilla

Combine sugar and corn syrup in pot. Dissolve cream of tartar in water and mix with sugar and syrup. Add vanilla. Cook to 265° (on candy thermometer). Don't stir—just pull!

Salt of the Earth

Courtesy of Riverwalk

Salt has always been one of Louisiana's priceless assets. Native American Indians replenished their supplies of this essential mineral at saline springs that abound in the southern part of the state. Salt was among the inducements for Daniel Coxe to launch his expedition to explore the northern shore of the Gulf of Mexico and the lower Mississippi River in 1698-1699. Rumors of a mysterious, giant underground source of rock salt "almost as clear as crystal" were cited as justification for the United States to buy the Louisiana Territory for fifteen million dollars in 1803.

Until the Civil War, the South had been producing very little of the salt that it needed. Louisiana had supplied only its local needs from a salt spring on Avery Island. In May, 1862, shafts were sunk on nearby Petit Anse Island, tapping an enormous deposit of rock salt that became the most important source of the Confederacy's salt supply. A packing plant built near the mine yielded millions of pounds monthly. Beef was prepared there for shipment throughout the south. Later that year, when New Orleans fell to the Union Navy, the mine was seized by Union forces, dealing a major blow to the Confederacy.

Future discoveries would reveal even more staggering deposits. Today we know that southern Louisiana is honeycombed with mammoth underground salt domes that contain a never ending supply of this mineral.

Filet Mignon Zingara

Submitted by Chef Daniel Bonnot

4	filet mignons (7 ounces each)
6 ounces	fresh mushrooms
4 ounces	marsala wine
6 ounces	smoked beef tongue, julienne cut
6 ounces	prosciutto, julienne cut
8 ounces	thickened brown veal stock

Sauté filet to desired doneness. Sauté mushrooms. Add marsala wine and reduce. Add smoked tongue, prosciutto and brown veal stock. Salt and pepper to taste. Cook until heated through. **Serves:** 4

Spanish Bean Soup

Submitted by Mrs. Solon Brinton Turman

1 pound	navy beans
2 bunches	fresh young collard greens, chopped fine
4 large	potatoes, quartered
½ pound	salt meat
1 pound	chorizos (Spanish sausage; if not available, use smoked sausage), cut into small pieces
2 pinches	saffron salt and pepper to taste

Soak beans overnight, add beans to chopped greens, potatoes, salt meat, saffron and sausage. Cover with water and let cook for about three hours or until beans are tender. Add salt and pepper to taste. **Serve:** 8-10

Red Beans and Rice on Monday

Courtesy of Riverwalk

Traditionally, red beans and rice are served in New Orleans on Monday, wash day in the old Creole or Cajun household. Before the days of automatic appliances, washing was a demanding chore, and the slow simmering of beans could go virtually unattended while the toil of the wash was completed. This plain and simple dish has become an epicurean delight, and its popularity has spread outside the home. Some local restaurants have this item on the menu every day.

The origins of the dish are somewhat shrouded in history. One theorist maintains that it is of Spanish colonial origin, pointing out that nearly the same dish is found in Andalusia, in Spain, under the name Moros y Cristianos, or Moors and Christians, the beans representing the Moors and the rice the Christians. Rice itself, indispensible to this dish, traveled to the Western world via the Moslem, or Moorish, culture of Andalusia. Even our word "rice" comes from the Arabic arruz.

Here's a basic recipe: Soak a pound of red beans overnight. The next day, add ham, pickled pork, or smoked sausage and simmer for several hours. When the beans are tender, add one medium onion chopped, at least one clove of minced garlic, and chopped bell pepper and celery to taste. A few bay leaves and some hot sauce are good, too. Simmer until all flavors are blended. Serve over hot rice.

Craig's Favorite Red Beans and Rice

Submitted by Chiqui Collier, Cookery N'Orleans Style Restaurant

1 pound	red beans
2 Tablespoons	olive oil
2 Tablespoons	bacon drippings
2 cloves	garlic, minced
1 medium	onion, minced
1 bunch	green onions and tops, sliced thin
1 medium	onion minced
½ medium	bell pepper, minced
4 pieces	celery with leaves, minced
1 Tablespoon	parsley
1 pound	ham seasoning (cubes)
1 piece	pickled meat (optional)
½ teaspoon	thyme
1	bay leaf
½ teaspoon	dried Italian seasoning
½ teaspoon	lemon pepper
2	chicken bouillon cubes

Soak the red beans in water overnight. Drain and rinse well.

In pressure cooker pot, heat olive oil and bacon drippings. Add garlic, onion, green onions, bell pepper, celery and parsley. Sauté about 5-8 minutes. Add remaining ingredients, including drained beans. Add enough water to cover beans by at least 1-inch. Pressure cook 25 minutes. Uncover. Continue to cook about 15 minutes to thicken. Serve over rice with French bread. **Serves:** 6 or more

Red Beans and Rice

Courtesy of Riverwalk

Quarter red beans, quarter rice
Little piece of salt meat to make it taste nice
Lend me the paper and tell me the time
My husband'll be by to pay you the dime.

Everybody in New Orleans eats red beans and rice at least once a week and traditionally on Monday. You see, Monday was wash day and the Creole mother always wanted to serve a hearty meal to her family even though she would spend hours scrubbing the wash on the washboard. (She had to boil the white clothes to keep them from being dingy because everything went out on the line and the neighbors would talk.) Well, the pot of beans could cook all day and if she put in enough water, it would be fine till supper time. Now, if you don't cook red beans right, they'll give you gas. So here in New Orleans, we cook them upside down so you only get hiccups.

Uncle Sidney's Red Beans

Submitted by Austin Leslie, Chez Helene Restaurant

2 pounds	red beans (fresh)
1 large	onion, diced
1 rib	celery, diced
8 toes	garlic, finely chopped
8 sprigs	parsley, chopped
1	bell pepper, finely chopped
2 pounds	pickle pork rib tips, or smoked shoulder of ham cubed, smoked ham hocks
1	baked ham bone (sawed in several places)
3	bay leaves
1 Tablespoon	thyme
	salt and pepper to taste
1 stick	butter
8 cups	cooked rice

Pick over beans before cleaning and remove any bruised or spotted ones. Soak in water overnight in a covered pot. Add diced onion to beans while they are soaking. The following day, strain and pour off water. Return beans and onion to pot. Add all remaining ingredients to pot, except salt, pepper, butter, and rice. Fill pot with water just to cover ingredients. Bring to boil and reduce to a simmer. Season to taste with salt and pepper. (Be careful with the salt.) Simmer for 2 to 2½ hours. When tender and creamy, add 1 stick of butter and stir in. Serve over boiled rice.

Hint: The butter improves texture of gravy.
Serves: 8 or more

Rice is Nice

Courtesy of Riverwalk

Rice was first grown in Asia and did not enter Europe until the eleventh century. In Louisiana, its cultivation started along the Mississippi River in French colonial times. It was not until after the Civil War, however, that it became such an important cash crop, its cultivation having spread far southwest of New Orleans, into Cajun country. By 1886, the first modern rice mill was built in the region, and three years later the state emerged as the leading producer of the crop in the United States. Louisiana is still close to the top, though the industry has spread to Texas, Arkansas, California, and other places.

Rice is the basis of much Creole and Cajun cooking—red beans and rice, shrimp stew over rice, and so forth. A sweet, cake-like confection called the calas and made from rice was a big seller for street vendors in New Orleans until our own times. Even non-Creole foods are frequently accompanied in the southern part of the state by rice, rather than potatoes, grits, or other starches. In fact, it has long been considered the mark of the true Cajun that he can look at the field of rice growing in the warm Louisiana sun and tell you exactly how much gravy it will take to cover it all.

Dirty Rice

Submitted by Jannie Lacour

2 cups	rice
1 pound	chicken livers
1 pound	chicken gizzards
	dash salt
	black pepper to taste
	cayenne pepper to taste
1 small	bell pepper, chopped
4 tails	green onion, chopped
1 small	head onion, chopped
6 pods	garlic, minced
	garlic salt to taste
1 pound	ground beef

Wash rice under hot tap water several times until milky water runs clear. Run some hot water into pot about an inch over rice. Bring to a boil, then put lid on and simmer for about 20 minutes checking for doneness. Put chicken livers and gizzards into another pot, cover with water and simmer for about 15 minutes on medium heat. Add salt, black pepper, cayenne pepper, bell pepper, green onion, half the chopped onion, garlic, and garlic salt leaving lid off. Cook for about 20 minutes and then cut up livers and gizzards or grind them up. Put ground beef into pot, put livers and gizzards back into pot and cook until done. Don't let all of the juices dry out. Put remaining onion into pot about 10 minutes before turning pot off. When finished, stir rice in. If dry add a tablespoon of shortening. **Serves:** 10

Mother's Riz Au Lait

Submitted by Alcée-Hymel Family

1 cup	cooked rice
2 cups	simmering milk
¾ cup	sugar
½ teaspoon	pure vanilla extract
	nutmeg

Add the rice to the simmering milk and cook on slow fire for four minutes. Add sugar, stir well, and cook for one minute. Remove from the heat and add the vanilla extract. Mix thoroughly and place in a dish to cool. Sprinkle top with nutmeg, and serve at room temperature. **Serves:** 4

The Legend of Gumbo

Submitted by The Gumbo Shop

On entering the pearly gates, a New Orleans Creole asked, "But, Monsieur, where is the pot of Gumbo? And the Jambalaya?" He was told that this was the land of milk and honey. The Creole replied, "Perhaps that 'spicier' place below will be more to my taste."

New Orleans, settled by the French in 1718, was ceded to the Spanish in 1766. These colonists eventually intermarried—their offspring, born in New Orleans, are Creoles. The Africans, West Indians and American Indians combined their traditional heritage and spices with the Creoles' to develop Creole food.

Most Gumbos contain one or two ingredients—filé and okra. The African word for okra is "gombo" and the Choctaw Indian word for filé, which is made from dried sassafras leaves, is "kombo." No one agrees on the exact origin of the word, which is perfectly all right because no one agrees on an exact recipe for Gumbo either. The final flavor usually depends on what is available in the kitchen—oysters, crabs, shrimp, chicken and/or sausage, etc.

Chicken and Seafood Gumbo

Submitted by Mrs. Carmen R. Ricard

1 cup	oil
1 cup	flour
1 cup	chopped onions
1 cup	chopped bell peppers
1 cup	chopped celery
6 quarts	water or chicken broth
1 large	fryer (3-4 pounds), cut into serving pieces
¼ cup	oil
1 pound	smoked sausage (sliced)
2	bay leaves
3 dozen	oysters
2 pounds	deveined shrimp
½ cup	chopped green onion tops
½ cup	chopped parsley salt and pepper to taste
1 Tablespoon	filé (optional)

Heat oil in a 6-8 quart pot, add flour and cook until dark brown. Add onions, bell pepper, and celery and cook until soft. Add water or chicken broth to roux, mix thoroughly and bring to a boil.

Sauté chicken in ¼ cup of oil. When chicken has browned, add to broth and let simmer. Sauté smoked sausage and add sausage and bay leaves to broth. When chicken is tender, add oysters, shrimp, green onions and parsley and cook 10-15 minutes (or until shrimp are cooked). Salt and pepper to taste. Filé may be added to pot when gumbo is cooked.

Serve gumbo over rice—filé may be sprinkled on by individuals. **Serves:** 12-14

Filé Gumbo

Courtesy of Riverwalk

Gumbo, of all the products of Louisiana cuisine, represents a most distinctive evolution of good cookery from African and Caribbean sources. Having received its name from an African word for okra, ngombo, it was at first customary to make this savory stew with okra as a thickening agent. Most often, an okra gumbo was a seafood gumbo.

Other gumbos came to be made with a different thickening agent, filé. Filé is a powder that used to be manufactured by the Choctaw Indians in Louisiana from the young and tender leaves of the sassafras plant, dried and pounded.

Here is a recipe with rather approximate measurements characteristic of Creole cooking: Prepare a roux by browning about a third of a cup of flour in oil in the oven or on top of the stove in a heavy skillet. Add quantities of chicken, sausages, ham, or other meats to your taste to a large pot of water and the roux. Add parsley, bay leaves, onions, cayenne, and other seasonings that you like. Slow boil or simmer for at least a couple hours. In the last few moments of boiling, add about two tablespoons of filé, which will add an extra degree of thickening and color to the dish, not to mention a uniquely savory flavor. Serve over rice.

Ideally, the gumbo should never be reheated as the filé tends to thin out.

Austin's Filé Gumbo

Submitted by Austin Leslie, Chez Helene

½ pound	margarine
1 rib	celery, chopped
1	onion, finely chopped
4 sprigs	parsley, finely chopped

½	green pepper, finely chopped
4 toes	garlic, finely chopped
½ cup	flour
1 gallon	shellfish stock or water
3	bay leaves
½ pound	smoked ham, diced
6	crabs (cleaned and quartered)
½ pound	hot sausage (¼-inch slices)
½ pound	smoked sausage (½-inch slices)
½ pound	shrimp (peeled and deveined, heads and shells reserve for stock)
1 Tablespoon	thyme
	salt and pepper to taste
2 Tablespoons	filé powder
	fresh cooked rice

Place margarine at bottom of a large soup pot. Add celery, onion, parsley, green pepper and garlic. Sauté and then simmer for 15 to 20 minutes over low heat. Add flour and stir constantly for 15 more minutes. Add stock or water and bay leaves. Heat over medium flame for 20 minutes. Stir in ham, crabs, sausages and cook for 30 minutes. Bring to a boil and keep stirring to avoid sticking. When pot returns to boil, add shrimp, thyme, salt and pepper. Allow to return to the boiling point again. Remove from heat and check salt and pepper, adding more if needed. Finally, stir in filé powder and serve immediately over fresh rice.

Serves: 10-12

Chicken or Turkey Gumbo

Submitted by Chiqui Collier, Cookery N'Orleans Style Restaurant

1 3-4 pound	broiler fryer, cut-up or leftover turkey drumstick, wings and turkey carcass
1 pound	okra, sliced
6 Tablespoons	bacon drippings
1 medium	onion, chopped
2 ribs	celery and leaves, chopped
2 toes	garlic, minced
½ medium	bell pepper, chopped
2 sprigs	parsley, minced
4 Tablespoons	bacon drippings
3 Tablespoons	flour
1½ pounds	country smoked sausage
1	bay leaf
1 teaspoon	thyme
	dash Tabasco®
	lemon pepper to taste
	salt (if necessary)
	cooked rice

Brown cut-up chicken in a little oleo and oil (or boil until tender with seasonings in water to cover or use leftover turkey drumstick, wings and turkey carcass). Boil in a large pot with any leftover gravy and water to cover for 2½ to 3 hours. Strain broth, remove bones and skin. Cut-up meat in large chunks.

Fry sliced okra in 6 Tablespoons bacon drippings for about 30 minutes (until it ceases to "rope").

Sauté onion, celery, garlic, bell pepper and parsley in 4 Tablespoons bacon drippings. Stir in flour and cook until golden brown. Add this to the large pot of strained broth along with the prepared okra. Slice and sauté the country sausage. Add this to the pot of broth. Add all seasonings and the reserved chicken or turkey. Simmer on low for 40 minutes. Serve in deep bowls over mounds of fluffy rice. **Serves: 8**

Origins of Jambalaya

Courtesy of Riverwalk

A red jambalaya (using tomato sauce) is characteristic of the Creoles while brown jambalaya is typical of the Cajuns. Both forms are influenced by the French, Spanish and Africans.

Jambalaya

Submitted by the Bergeron Family

1 pound	smoked sausage
3	pork chops, boned
2	chicken breasts, boned
3 Tablespoons	cooking oil
½ cup	onions
½ cup	bell pepper
½ cup	celery
1 bunch	shallots
6 cloves	garlic
3 Tablespoons	parsley
3 cups	water
2 cups	rice

Cut sausage into thin slices. Cut pork chops and chicken breasts into small pieces.

Place oil in heavy pot and heat. Add sausage, pork and chicken. Cook until brown, then add onions, pepper, celery, shallots, garlic, and parsley and sauté until tender. Add water and bring to a boil. Add rice and cook until liquid is absorbed, then lower heat, cover and cook about 15 more minutes.
Serves: 6 or more

Gumbo Shop Jambalaya

Submitted by Richard Stewart, The Gumbo Shop

Jambalaya derives its name from "Jambon" the French word for ham. Ham is almost always an ingredient, along with any combination of sausage, shrimp, chicken, etc. It is similar to the Spanish dish "Paella."

¼ cup	cooking oil
½ pound	smoked sausage sliced
½ pound	ham, diced
1 cup	onion, chopped
1 cup	bell pepper, chopped
1 cup	celery, chopped
1 cup	green onion, chopped
2 cloves	garlic, minced
1 can (16 ounces)	tomatoes drained, reserving liquid
1 teaspoon	thyme
1 teaspoon	black pepper
1 teaspoon	salt
1 cup	converted rice
1½ cups	stock or water
1½ Tablespoons	Worcestershire sauce
2 pounds	peeled shrimp

Place oil in a large heavy dutch oven and sauté sausage and ham until lightly browned. Remove from pot and set aside. Sauté onion, bell pepper, celery, green onion and garlic in meat drippings until tender. Add tomatoes, thyme, pepper and salt. Cook 5 minutes. Stir in rice. Mix together liquid from tomatoes, stock, and Worcestershire to equal 2 cups and add to sautéed vegetables. Bring to a boil, reduce to a simmer, add raw shrimp, ham and sausage and cook uncovered, stirring occasionally for about 30 minutes or until rice and shrimp are done. **Serves:** 6-8

Shrimp Jambalaya

Submitted by Lillie Petit Gallagher, "Oilfield Journal"

2	onions
1 Tablespoon	butter
1 Tablespoon	flour
1 sprig each	thyme and bay leaf
2 sprigs	parsley
2	finely chopped garlic cloves
½ teaspoon	chili pepper
3	tomatoes, chopped fine, reserve juice of tomato
3 quarts	oyster broth or water
3 pounds	peeled shrimp, boiled
1½ cups	rice
	salt to taste
	pepper to taste

Chop onions very fine, and put them in a saucepan to brown with butter. After a few minutes add flour and stir well. Then add chopped thyme, bay leaf, parsley and garlic. Let all of this fry five minutes longer and be careful not to let it burn or brown too much. Add chili pepper, tomatoes, and tomato juice. Let all brown or simmer for ten minutes longer. When cooked, add oyster broth or water. Let all boil well and then add shrimp. Let the mixture boil again for five minutes and add rice. Add salt and pepper to taste. Mix all well, and let boil for one half hour or longer until rice is cooked and all is thoroughly mixed. Stir occasionally. **Serves: 8**

Pasta Jambalaya

Submitted by Ralph Brennan, Mr. B's

½ ounce	melted butter
1½ ounces	andouille sausage
1 ounce	cooked duck breast
1 ounce	raw chicken breast sliced thin
3	shrimp (21/25 size)
2 Tablespoons	diced onions
2 Tablespoons	diced pepper, red and green
3 ounces	veal stock
2 Tablespoons	ripe tomatoes
½ teaspoon	chopped garlic
	pinch red pepper flakes
	garlic to taste
½ teaspoon	Creole seasoning®
2½ ounces	cold sweet butter pieces
4 ounces	spinach pasta (cooked)

Melt butter in pan. Add andouille, duck meat, chicken, shrimp, onion, garlic, and pepper to hot sauté pan. Sauté over high flame, stirring with fork and shaking pan. When shrimp are half cooked through (about 2 minutes) add veal stock, tomatoes, and seasoning. Reduce by ⅓.

Swirl in cold butter pieces, continuously stirring with fork and rotating sauté pans until all butter is incorporated (sauce should be smooth and light). Place warm pasta in bowl, pour jambalaya over and serve immediately. **Serves:** 1

Chicken/Andouille Jambalaya

Submitted by Lois Comeaux

1 small	chicken (2½ pounds) deboned and chopped
1 pound	andouille sliced thin
1 ounce	oil
1 large	onion, chopped
4 cloves	garlic, chopped
1 large	bell pepper, chopped
4-6 stalks	celery chopped
	Cajun seasoning® for poultry to taste
2 cups	rice
2½ cups	chicken stock (or water)
½ bunch	green onions, chopped
½ cup	fresh parsley, chopped

As you debone chicken, place bone, skin, wings, back, gizzards and neck in water and boil to make stock.

Sauté sliced andouille in oil for about 5-10 minutes. Remove. In same pan, sauté chopped chicken for about 5-10 minutes. Remove. In same pan, sauté chopped onion, garlic, bell pepper and celery. Return chicken and andouille when vegetables have cooked down. Add seasoning, rice and stock. Cook 30-35 minutes on medium flame. Add green onions and parsley and cook 10 minutes longer. **Serves:** 6-8

Dancing the Shrimp on the Platforms

Courtesy of Riverwalk

In the early times, those unlucky enough not to live near sources of fresh shrimp, as southern Louisianians do, usually had to make do with the preserved variety. Shrimp were first canned commercially in the state in 1867. But drying the shrimp was the most popular way of preserving them in the latter half of the 1800's.

Large platforms were built on pilings in the swamps, carrying both homes and shrimp-drying facilities. One of the earliest and longest-lived platforms was Manila Village, established in 1873 by Chinese and Filipinos. Other platforms were Basa Basa, Leon Rojas, Bayou Cholas, and Bayou Bruleau. These settlements were an amazingly varied mixture of Creole, Mexican, South American Indian, Chinese, Filipino, and others.

The shrimp were boiled in salt water. Then they were raked and turned in the sun until thoroughly dried. The heads and hulls were removed by a process called "dancing the shrimp," in which the whole population of the platform, men, women, and children, with their feet wrapped in burlap, treaded rhythmically on the shrimp while chanting songs.

Manila Village was abandoned after a big hurricane in 1965. Only a single ramshackle structure remains today. But dried shrimp are still available in small cellophane packets, and the area in which fresh, chilled shrimp may be sold has been expanded greatly by modern refrigeration.

Ann's Barbecue Shrimp

Submitted by Ann C. Rogers

3 medium	onions
2 cloves	garlic
1 heaping Tablespoon	McCormick Italian Seasoning®
1 teaspoon	salt
¼ cup	white vinegar
4 or 5 dashes	Tabasco® sauce
3 Tablespoons	black pepper
2 Tablespoons	red or cayenne pepper
1 small bottle	Italian dressing
	juice of 1 lemon
2 small	cans tomato sauce
3 or 4 sticks	of margarine
3 or 4 pounds	of headless shrimp

Put all ingredients except margarine and shrimp in blender and liquify.

In a 13 × 9-inch pan melt margarine and stir the contents of the blender into the melted butter.

Take 3 or 4 pounds of headless shrimp and place in the sauce and stir to coat all shrimp, then place in the oven and bake at 375 to 400° for 30 minutes. Test for doneness (shrimp will turn pink), as the cooking time will vary depending on the size of the shrimp. Do not peel the shrimp before cooking. Serve with fresh French bread and dip in the sauce. The bread is almost as good as the shrimp. **Serves: 6-8**

Shrimp Rémoulade

Submitted by Chiqui Collier, Cookery N'Orleans Style Restaurant

4 Tablespoons	prepared yellow mustard
4 Tablespoons	prepared horseradish
½ cup	tarragon vinegar
2 Tablespoons	ketchup
1 Tablespoon	paprika
1 teaspoon	salt
1 large clove	garlic
1 cup	salad oil
1 bunch	green onions with tops
4 ribs	celery with leaves
½ teaspoon	cayenne pepper (or to taste)
5 pounds	boiled shrimp, peeled and deveined

Place all ingredients except shrimp in blender and purée. Store in refrigerator in a tightly covered glass jar. To serve, allow boiled shrimp to marinate in sauce at least 4 hours. Serve over shredded lettuce. **Variation:** May be served over a wedge of iceberg lettuce and topped with chopped hard boiled egg. **Serves:** 10

Creole Cream Cheese: A Dying Art?

Submitted by Alcée-Hymel Family

One of the most prized of local delicacies is Creole cream cheese, which, years ago was made from clabbered milk. Unfortunately, very few local dairies still produce it, but the demand continues. (After suspending manufacturing of Creole cream cheese, a major dairy products firm was forced by popular response to reintroduce it.)

In order to make your own Creole cream cheese, you must first allow the milk to clabber by draining water from the cream. The clabber is placed in a long bag of muslin, tied tightly and hung out overnight in a cool place. The next day, the cheese is beaten until light and placed in an appropriate container and chilled. Just before serving, fresh sweet cream is poured over it. It usually is served with sugar and fruit and can be made into a frozen dessert. Historically the French serve Creole cream cheese with sugar and nutmeg; the Germans serve it with onions and call it Schmier Kase.

Frozen Cream Cheese

Submitted by The Alcée-Hymel Family

2 containers (14-ounces each)	Creole cream cheese with their cream
1 cup	undiluted evaporated milk
1 cup	granulated sugar
½ teaspoon	vanilla
1	egg white

Mash the cream cheese with the milk. Add sugar, then vanilla and fold in the stiffly beaten egg white. Pour into freezer container and freeze. **Serves: 6**

Louisiana Creole Cream Cheese Dessert

Submitted by Chef Buster, Chef Buster's Restaurant

The recipe that follows is extremely old and dates back to when the plantation and the river were "King and Queen of the Mighty Mississippi."

My grandparents came to this country from Europe and were employed at a plantation up the river from New Orleans. During the summer months, as I was told by my Grandma, it was hard to prepare foods that should be cooled, especially desserts. As she went on to tell me, this dessert was always enjoyed on the plantation, and more often on a long Sunday afternoon when company had arrived.

When asked "Well Grandma, how did you keep it cold?", she would say that when the riverboat left New Orleans and came up river, they would have big blocks of ice that were wrapped in tarpaulin cloth and then straw. In great haste, the workers would bring the ice to the plantation.

During these times, this plantation was built high off the ground because of the spring floods. When the ice was brought to the plantation, it was put in a cement brick house that was built underneath the plantation house for such occasions. The ice was once again wrapped with the tarpaulin and straw.

My Grandma said that everything used for this recipe came from the plantation with the exception of the West Indies Rum or vanilla. It was easy to prepare the desserts and if the strawberries were out of season, there were always the fields of wild strawberries.

After dessert was prepared with the Creole fixins' Grandma would bring it to the ice block. She would chip away at the ice until she could fit the bowl of cream cheese snuggly home.

Louisiana Creole
Cream Cheese Dessert

Submitted by Chef Buster's Restaurant

12 ounces	granulated sugar
1½ pints	strawberries or black-berries, blueberries, etc.
28 ounces	Creole cream cheese or 2 14-ounce containers
1 ounce	of rum or vanilla extract
1½ cups	heavy cream, whipped until peaked

Take 6 ounces of the sugar and mix together well with the fresh fruit. Place them under refrigeration until you are ready to use.

In a bowl, mix the Creole cream cheese and the remaining sugar together. Add rum or vanilla extract. With a rubber spatula gently fold in the whipped cream. When all the whipped cream has been added, place the mixture into 3-ounce paper cups and put into the freezer. When the Creole cream cheese has hardened remove from the cups and place into a small dessert bowl and cover with the fresh fruit and serve. **Serves:** 6

Chicory, That Savory Root

Courtesy of Riverwalk

Chicory is a perennial plant native to Europe, Chicorium intybus is its Latin name. It has bright blue flowers, delicate leaves, and roots that are used roasted and ground as a substitute or additive for coffee. The leaves of the closely related Chicorium endivia are the tasty endive encountered in more adventurous salads.

Although chicory has been used in Europe to strengthen the flavor of coffee almost as far back as that beverage's acceptance there, it wasn't until the Civil War that it became so popular in this region of the United States. It was the scarcities resulting from that bloody and seemingly endless struggle that really established chicory here. Month after month of tight blockade of New Orleans and other Southern ports by the Union Navy, inevitably resulted in severe shortages of coffee and all kinds of other staple goods. The less coffee people had on hand, the more chicory they were inclined to mix with it in order to stretch the supply. A popular blend was two parts chicory and one part coffee. Later, confederates were reduced to chicory alone, if they were lucky, otherwise parched rye, sweetened with sorghum molasses. Toward the end of the war, they were drinking a brew of blackened sweet potatoes (yams).

To this day, local-born people still ask for "Northern coffee" when they want their java without chicory.

Weak Coffee

Submitted by Josephine Ferguson

When I went to California one time I had dinner with a man who had taught at Tulane. At that time, he was a professor at the University of California. He told everyone at the table that the coffee in New Orleans was like lye. Well, I sure missed our good coffee that night because when the coffee was served it tasted like weak tea.

Coffee Mousse

Submitted by Roland A. Chiara

16	marshmallows
½ cup	strong coffee with chicory
1 Tablespoon	granulated sugar
½ pint	whipped cream
1 teaspoon	vanilla

Melt marshmallows in hot coffee, cool. Beat in sugar. Add whipped cream and vanilla. Place in sherbet glasses and chill. Serve with tiny topping of whipped cream. **Serves:** 6

Café Au Lait

Submitted by Commander's Palace

Café Au Lait, a New Orleans institution, is a thick, rich coffee concoction natives drink at breakfast, all day long, and after dinner with sugar, instead of dessert. Usually, equal parts of milk (or cream) heated just to boiling and New Orleans chicory coffee are used, though this is a matter of taste. It's nice sometimes to serve it with a little coffee ceremony, simultaneously pouring coffee from a pot in one hand and boiling milk or cream from a pot in the other hand.

Food For Thought

Courtesy of Riverwalk

Everybody knows how good the sandwiches are at Masperos on Chartres Street, but under Pierre Masperos' management at the City Exchange on St. Louis Street, the world renowned New Orleans gumbo was created. New Orleans gumbo is a combination of the Marseilles bouillabaisse, Creole imagination, African okra, and Choctaw filé powder.

The City Exchange was also the first bar to serve the free lunch. The menu consisted of soup, a piece of beef or ham with potatoes, meat pie and oyster patties. This was served with whatever drink you ordered until the depression came and the free lunch became too expensive to give away to the long lines of people who had just enough money for one drink.

Oak Alley Plantation Restaurant's Chicken and Andouille Gumbo

Submitted by Joanne Amorte, Oak Alley Plantation

1½ cups	all purpose flour
1½ cups	vegetable oil
2 cups	onion, chopped
1 cup	celery, chopped
1 cup	green pepper, chopped
½ cup	green onion, chopped
¼ cup	parsley, chopped
2	bay leaves
2 gallons	chicken stock (use broth from boiled chicken and add water to make 2 gallons)
3 pounds	smoked sausage, cut
1 pound	andouille, cut salt, black pepper, cayenne to taste
2 whole	chickens, boiled and deboned filé powder to taste

Make a roux by slowly browning flour in the hot oil. This is a slow process and must be stirred constantly. When roux is medium brown, add onions, celery, green pepper, green onions, parsley, and bay leaves. Cook on low flame until vegetables are soft. Add 1½ gallons hot chicken stock to roux. Boil 15 minutes. Add smoked sausage and andouille. Cook over medium-low flame for four hours. Add more chicken stock to get desired consistency. Stir in salt, pepper and cayenne. Add the cooked chicken and cook for another hour. Just before serving, stir in filé and serve immediately. **Serves:** 20

Meat Pies

Submitted by Jannie Lacour

Filling:

1 pound	ground beef
1 pound	ground pork
bunch	green onions
1 small	bell pepper
1 small	onion
6 pods	garlic
	cayenne pepper to taste
	black pepper to taste
	garlic salt to taste
	season salt to taste
2 Tablespoons	flour

Mix ground beef and ground pork into pot. Chop up green onion, bell pepper, onion, garlic, and add cayenne pepper, black pepper, garlic salt and season salt. Cook on medium heat, stirring often to keep meat from sticking. Cook for about 30-40 minutes until done. If meat is extra fatty, take off some of the drippings because the meat pies will be too greasy. Stir in a tablespoon or two of flour after you turn heat off. Let meat chill. After the filling has chilled put a tablespoon or two into crust.

Crust:

⅓ cup	of shortening
1	egg well beaten
¾ cup	of milk
2 cups	self rising flour
	oil for frying

Mix shortening, egg, and milk well, adding flour a little at a time. Knead well and roll out dough very thin using a saucer for a round cutting guide. Now spoon in a tablespoon or two of filling into center and along edge and fold over and make edges meet. Firm edges with fork. Drop in deep fat and cook until golden brown. Drain and serve hot. **Yield:** 10 or more pies, depending on size

Oyster Soup with Pastry Dome

Submitted by Commander's Palace Restaurant

½ medium	onion, finely chopped
1 stalk	celery, finely chopped
2 cloves	garlic, minced
1	bay leaf
2	green onions, finely chopped
¼ pound (1 stick)	butter
½ cup	all purpose flour
5 cups	fresh oyster liquid*
2 Tablespoons	Worcestershire sauce
1 pint	freshly shucked oysters with liquid salt and pepper to taste
3 Tablespoons	finely chopped fresh parsely
1 pound	puff pastry, defrosted, but still cold

Sauté onion, celery, garlic, bay leaf and green onions in butter until tender. Add flour and stir until mixture comes away from sides of pan. Cook over low heat for a few minutes.

Add oyster broth, drained from the fresh oysters, and whisk until smooth. Add Worcestershire and cook over low heat for 30 minutes. Add drained oysters and salt and pepper to taste. Bring to a boil. Remove from heat and stir in parsley.

Preheat oven to 375°.

Divide soup into 6 individual oven-proof bowls. Roll out puff pastry thinly on floured surface and cut into 6 rounds the same diameter as tops of soup bowls. Arrange one round on top of each serving of soup. Do not prick pastry with fork. Bake in the preheated oven for 20 minutes, or until pastry is puffed and golden brown. Serve immediately.

*Note: If there is not enough oyster liquid drained from the oysters to measure 5 cups, add water to the oysters and liquid to make the necessary 5 cups. Strain oysters when liquid is needed.

Serves: 6

Turtle Soup Au Sherry

Submitted by Delmonico Restaurant

1½ to 2 pounds	turtle meat, finely diced
2 quarts	water
2 stalks	celery, sliced
1 onion,	chopped
1 clove	garlic, minced
¼ teaspoon	salt
¼ cup	olive oil
¼ cup	vegetable oil
¼ cup	allpurpose flour
1½ cups	chopped leeks or green onions
1 cup	chopped tomato
	salt to taste
	dry sherry
4	hardcooked eggs, chopped

Combine turtle meat, water, celery, onion, garlic, and ¼ teaspoon salt in a 4-quart Dutch oven; heat to boiling. Reduce heat; simmer 30 minutes, skimming top if necessary.

Heat oil in a medium skillet until warm. Stir in flour; cook over low heat, stirring constantly, until flour is browned. Add leeks and tomato; cook, stirring frequently, until leeks are lightly browned. Stir flour mixture into hot broth; cook until thickened and bubbly. Add salt to taste; stir in additional water if soup is too thick.

Ladle soup into serving bowls; stir about 1 teaspoon sherry into each, and top with chopped egg.
Yield: 8 servings

Po-Boy

Courtesy of Riverwalk

Long before the national popularity of the hero or submarine sandwich, New Orleans was enjoying the Poor Boy, a sandwich made from crusty French bread stuffed with almost anything the cook had on hand—ham, cheese, fried fish, you name it.

One theory proposes that the Po-Boy was named after the French word pourboire, meaning "tip" or "gratuity," because of the diminutive price (some cost only five cents).

The classic Po-Boy combination is roast beef on a loaf of French bread soaked with the thick natural gravy of the beef, "dressed" with shredded lettuce, tomato and mayonnaise.

Roast Beef Po-Boy

Courtesy of Riverwalk

1 loaf	French bread (fresh as possible)
⅔ cup	rich, thick natural gravy
	mayonnaise
¾ cup	shredded lettuce
4-6 slices	roast beef (very thin)
3 slices	tomato
	plenty of napkins (to catch drippings)

Warm bread for a few minutes. Split lengthwise and soak in gravy. Cover with generous layer of mayonnaise (bottom half only). Sprinkle lettuce over mayonnaise, then add meat. Top with thinly sliced tomatos. Cover with top half of bread and serve. **Serves:** 1 hungry person or 2 moderately hungry people

The Po-Boy Sandwich

Submitted by Natchez House Restaurant

During the Great Depression of the late 1920s and early 1930s, economic hard times hit the United States. New Orleans was no exception, but here, in our city of friendly and caring people, local restauranteurs responded by creating a meal that almost any "poor boy" could afford. A tasty loaf of French bread was sliced lengthwise and a generous portion of mashed potatoes, potato salad, home fries or whatever potatoes the chef had made that day, was heaped in the middle and covered with gravy. This filling meal was sold for only 5 cents. Hence the name, Po-Boy Sandwich.

At the Natchez House Restaurant, we call our potato Po-Boy the Ninth Ward Special. Although no longer a nickel, it's a very economical way to get a great meal.

Natchez House Potato Po-Boy

Submitted by Natchez House Restaurant

½ loaf	French bread, split, heated and dressed with mayonnaise
layer	of mashed potatoes
layer	of potato salad
layer	of french fries

Soak with roast beef gravy and trimmings. Add layers of potatoes. **Serves: 1**

The Story of the Poor Boy

Submitted by Mel Leavitt, Historian, Author and TV Commentator

It is a huge, sturdy, simple sandwich.

You take a one-pound loaf of French bread fresh baked that morning, downy soft on the inside with a crispy-crunchy crust. You split it lengthwise and fill it, nice and sloppy, with six to seven slices of roast beef, lettuce, tomatoes, pickles and mayonnaise.

Voilà! You have a Po-Boy sandwich.

Variations are sold in other parts of the nation. It is difficult to tell which came first—the Po-Boy, the Submarine (Eastern seaboard), the Hero (New York City), the Cuban (Florida), Grinders (New England), or Hoagies (Philadelphia).

In New Orleans, the Po-Boy is a culinary delicacy because there is no other way you can eat so much food for so little. Besides, fresh French bread is a meal in itself.

That's why its inventor Benny Martin, a Cajun poor boy from Raceland, Louisiana, is considered a local hero. He arrived in the big city in 1914, a poor, French-speaking waif, and began working at odd jobs in the French Market.

At first, Benny and his brother Clovis were streetcar conductors who scarcely knew their way around the corner. In 1919, Benny married Augusta Punch, a young lass from tiny Lockport, and they began saving their nickels and silver dimes. By 1922, they had enough to buy a hole in the wall across from the French Market (Ursulines at North Peters). With brother Clovis, they opened Martin Brothers.

This local shrine was about twenty-five feet long with mirrored walls, good food, low prices and no trimmings. Eight rotating stools stood at three-foot intervals. Pork chops were 10 cents. Oysters 40 cents a dozen, raw. With these prices the Martin Brothers were fighting the Depression before there was one. The Martins took care of the poor, even when they couldn't pay. When Streetcar Union 194 went on strike, Benny and Clovis fed the men free until the strike was over.

That's how they named the Poor-Boy or Po-Boy, Sandwich. Half a loaf—15 cents. And talk about production; over 1,000 loaves of French bread were consumed every twenty-four hours. The Poor Boys' restaurant bustled day and night.

When the Depression hit, small businesses folded right and left. The Martin Brothers just got bigger. In 1931, they built a new restaurant at 2000 St. Claude, at the corner of Touro Street. They employed 38 waiters and waitresses. On Mardi Gras they used more than 3,000 loaves. "The miracle of the loaves and the fixin's," it was called. Martin Brothers boomed until the day Benny retired, on June 18, 1941.

Today, you can buy a Po-Boy sandwich at a wide variety of restaurants, including the pricey ones where the menu is written in French. This big, gooey, poor man's banquet is a New Orleans institution, like Creole gumbo, oysters Rockefeller, café au lait and beignets.

When Benny's granddaughter Sharyn Ann was married in 1969, Pawpaw and Mamère (Benny and Gus) celebrated their fiftieth wedding anniversary the same week. Benny rented the biggest hall he could find—Gallier Hall, once City Hall, and the Martins held a family-style reception. More than 1,000 friends, kith and kin showed up.

Benny summed it up neatly. "As you can see, mes amis, I'm a Po-Boy no mo'."

Chapter V

Reminiscence...A Little New Orleans Nostalgia

New Orleans "Nostalgia" is alive and well. Memories related to us by local Orleanians include everything from reminiscences about the River, songs of old time street vendors, to a grandchild's memories of "booze in the bathtub." These stories led to recipes that are some of the best to be found anywhere.

Through the Eyes of a Nun

Courtesy of Riverwalk

Sister Madeleine Hachard arrived in New Orleans in 1727 with a contingent of Ursulines who had been sent under a contract with the Company of the Indies. She wrote to her family back in France and described the people of New Orleans as they were at that time, as well as painted a verbal picture of the city.

"Our town is very handsome, well constructed and regularly built, as much as I could judge on the day of our arrival; for ever since that day we have remained cloistered in our dwelling. The streets are large and straight. The houses well built, with upright joists, the interstices filled with mortar, and the exterior white-washed with lime. In the interior they are wainscoted. The roofs of the houses are covered with shingles which are cut in the shape of slates, and one must know this to believe it, for they all have the appearance and beauty of slate. The colonists are very proud of their capital. Suffice it to say, they sing here a song in the streets to the effect that this town is as fine a sight as Paris. . .I do not, however, speak of the manners of the laity, but am told that their habits are corrupt and scandalous. There are, however, a great number of honest people, and one does not see any of those girls who were said to have been deported on compulsion. . .The women here are extremely ignorant as to the means of securing their salvation, but they are very expert in the art of displaying their beauty. There is so much luxury in this town that there is no distinction among the classes so far as dress goes. The magnificence of display is equal to all. Most of them reduce themselves and their family to a hard lot of living at home on nothing but sagamite, and flaunt abroad in robes of velvet and damask, ornamented with the most costly ribbons. They paint and rouge to hide the ravages of time, and wear on their faces, as embellishment, small black patches."

"New Orleans" Pound Cake

Submitted by Councilman Jim Singleton

1 cup	butter
2 cups	sugar
6	eggs
4 cups	flour
2 teaspoons	baking powder
pinch	of salt
pinch	of baking soda
1 cup	milk
1 teaspoon	vanilla

Cream butter and sugar, then add eggs, one at a time. Mix together flour, baking powder, salt and soda. Alternate sifted dry ingredients and milk to butter-egg mixture. Add vanilla. Bake in a deep greased pan for one and one-half hours at about 325° to 350°. When done, turn upside-down on rack, removing pan. Let cool, then serve. **Serves:** 12

Chants of Old New Orleans

Submitted by the Alcée-Hymel Family

Some of the most memorable and colorful sights and sounds of old New Orleans came from street vendors as they sold their wares and services—everyone from the chimney sweep to the shaved ice man had his own special cry.

People could almost tell the season by the vegetables and fruits carried by the vendors as they heard "cantaloupe lady, fresh to the rind," "blackberries lady, fresh from the vine."

There was the clothes pole man, the charcoal man, the candy man, the praline lady, the rice cake lady, the shaving cake man, the knife sharpener man and even the fresh eggs man. They offered a medley as well as a service, no longer found today, door-to-door delivery with a smile and a song!

The Waffle Man

Submitted by Carolyn Casey

In the Ninth Ward on Royal and St. Ferdinand, the waffle man would come down the street. He would blow a bugle and let you know that he had waffles.

Blackberry Lady

Submitted by Pat McClusky

This is a chant that I remember as a boy in New Orleans. It was said by the fruit vendor, and I remember it like it was yesterday.

"Blackberry Lady"

"Blackberry Lady"

"Watermelons red and ripe"

Old-Fashioned Three Layer Jam Cake

Submitted by Nan Simonson

1 cup	butter
1 cup	sugar
5	egg yolks
1 cup	strawberry jam
1 cup	apricot jam
1 cup	seedless blackberry jam (or jelly)
3 cups	all purpose flour
1 Tablespoon	cinnamon
½ teaspoon	nutmeg
1 Tablespoon	baking soda
1 cup	buttermilk
1 Tablespoon	baking soda
1 cup	chopped walnuts (optional)
5	egg whites, stiffly beaten

Cream butter and sugar until fluffy and light. Beat egg yolks well and add to above mixture. Mix well. Add the jams and mix well. Sift flour, cinnamon and nutmeg together. Dissolve soda in buttermilk. Add flour mixture alternately with buttermilk into creamed mixture. Stir in nuts. Beat egg whites until stiff and fold into batter gently. Bake in three greased and floured 9-inch baking pans for 35 to 40 minutes at 350°. Cool before frosting.

Frosting:

1 cup	butter
3 cups	confectioners sugar
4 Tablespoons	milk
1 teaspoon	vanilla

Mix ingredients and beat 10 minutes until creamy. Cover layers of cake, stack them and frost top and sides. **Yield:** 1 3-layer cake

Celebration Dessert

Submitted by Commander's Palace Restaurant

16 ounces	**French vanilla ice cream, softened**

Raspberry sauce:

1 pint	**fresh or frozen raspberries (puréed)**
½ cup	**sugar**

Raspberry filling:

1 pint	**whipping cream**
¾ cup	**raspberry sauce**

Chocolate frosting:

2 cups	**whipping cream**
½ cup	**sugar**
¾ cup	**semi-sweet cocoa powder**
4 ounces	**brandy**

Line the inside of 4 10-ounce paper cups with softened ice cream, molding it around the inside of the cup about ½-inch thick, leaving the center empty. Freeze until ice cream is hard.

To make raspberry sauce: combine raspberries and sugar in a saucepan. Bring to a boil and reduce to simmer for two minutes. Reserve some sauce to pour over slices of Celebration Dessert.

To make raspberry filling: Beat whipping cream until it forms stiff peaks. Add the raspberry sauce (reserving some) and beat again to stiff peaks. Fill the center of the cups with this filling and freeze again until very hard.

Turn the paper cups upside down under cold running water until they release the dessert and quickly slip onto individual chilled serving plates. Freeze again and pipe out the frosting over the dessert and down sides in a decorative pattern. Pipe out small stars or "kisses" all around the base.

Store in freezer until ready to serve. Allow to sit out.

When ready to serve, add brandy to reserved raspberry sauce and flame, pour over dessert. **Serves:** 4

Belle Cala! Tout Chaud!

Courtesy of Riverwalk

Under the cry, "Belle cala, tout chaud," a delicious rice cake was sold by the oldtime street vendors of New Orleans. It was always eaten with the morning cup of café au lait. The cala lady was a familiar figure on city streets until our own century. She usually was a black woman who carried the dainty and hot calas in a basket on her head. Her call penetrated the early morning air, as sleepers stirred from their dreams in anticipation of the delicious morning treat.

This custom is now long gone, but here is a recipe: Bring three cups of water to a hard boil, add half a cup of rice, and boil until mushy and soft. Cool, mash well, and add a half cake of compressed yeast or the dry yeast equivalent. Set to rise overnight. In the morning, add three beaten eggs, a half cup of sugar, three tablespoons of flour, and a half teaspoon of nutmeg. Set to rise for fifteen minutes more. Fry by the large spoonfuls in hot oil to a golden brown. Sprinkle with powdered sugar. The recipe also may be adapted for use with rice flour, omitting all but one tablespoon of wheat flour.

Calas are not to be confused with beignets, which are not made of rice.

Calas

Submitted by Alcée-Hymel Family

2	eggs beaten
1 cup	self-rising flour
1 cup	milk
2 cups	cold cooked rice
⅛ teaspoon	nutmeg
	oil for frying

Combine eggs, flour, milk, rice and nutmeg. Blend well. Spoon small amount of mixture on hot, slightly greased skillet. Cake should be small and thin. Brown on both sides, turning only once. Sprinkle with confectioners sugar. **Yield:** 8-10 calas.

Legends of the River

Submitted by Mary Desimone

I remember when I was a little girl, my Mother and Father would take me for a walk along the river. My Mother carried a basket on her arm which she called her market basket. One of the wharves we visited was occupied by the United Fruit Company. They unloaded bananas there from large ships. I remember my Father would talk to the men that were doing the unloading and they would fill my Mother's basket with bananas. They were the most beautiful bananas I have ever seen. Then we would walk along the river on the wharf until we came to the Esplanade Ferry Landing. My Father had a friend called Johnny Killian who had a catfish line set out in the river. My Father would buy the biggest fish he had. I will never forget how everyone seemed so happy in those days. There was always someone walking along the river that you could talk to. We lived in the Ninth Ward on Montegue Street and spent many happy days on the river.

Bananas Foster

Submitted by Brennan's Restaurant

This is one of Brennan's most famous and most popular desserts. It's really quite simple to prepare. Wait until the rum gets hot, so that you get a good flame when it's ignited. This can also be prepared over a stove burner, then brought to the dinner table and flamed.

4 Tablespoons	butter
1 cup	brown sugar
½ teaspoon	cinnamon
4 Tablespoons	banana liqueur
4	bananas, cut in half lengthwise, then halved
¼ cup	rum (approximately)
4 scoops	vanilla ice cream

Melt the butter over an alcohol burner in a flambé pan or attractive skillet. Add the sugar, cinnamon, and banana liqueur and stir to mix. Heat for a few minutes, then place the halved bananas in the sauce and sauté until soft and slightly browned. Add the rum and allow it to heat well, then tip the pan so that the flame from the burner causes the sauce to light. Allow the sauce to flame until it dies out, tipping the pan with a circular motion to prolong the flaming.

Serve over vanilla ice cream. First lift the bananas carefully out of the pan and place four pieces over each portion of ice cream, then spoon the hot sauce from the pan over the top. **Serves:** 4

Banana Bread

Submitted by Austin Leslie, Chez Helene Restaurant

2 cups	all purpose flour (unbleached and sifted)
1 teaspoon	baking soda
½ teaspoon	salt
1 teaspoon	cinnamon
½ cup	butter (softened)
1 cup	sugar
2 large	eggs
2 large	bananas (mashed)
⅓ cup	milk
1 teaspoon	lemon juice

Preheat oven to 350°. Sift the flour, baking soda, salt and cinnamon. Cream butter and add sugar, beat well. To the butter and sugar, add the eggs and bananas and mix well. Combine the milk and lemon juice and add to the egg-banana mixture. Fold dry ingredients by the ½ cup into liquid ingredients. Fold well after each ½ cup of dry ingredients. Pour batter into buttered 9 × 5 × 3 inch pan and bake at 350° for 1 hour. **Serves:** 4-6

Legend of the "Facts of the Eiffel Tower"

Submitted by Daniel Bonnot, Restaurant de la Tour Eiffel*

In 1981, engineers discovered that the restaurant perched 562 feet above the Eiffel Tower in Paris was causing the structure to sag, and they ordered it removed. It was then that Hotelier, John Onorio and French Chef, Daniel Bonnot began a four year quest to bring the restaurant to New Orleans, a city with strong ties to France. The restaurant's walls, floor and ceiling were dismantled into 2,000 carefully labeled pieces and packed into a 40 ft. long crate. The contents of this crate have been reassembled into what is now a landmark on St. Charles Avenue in New Orleans—"Restaurant de la Tour Eiffel."

* The restaurant is now closed.

Roti De Porc Braise Au Lait De Chevre (Roast Pork Loin Braised in Goat's Milk)

Submitted by Chef Daniel Bonnot

4	leeks
2 pounds	boneless pork loin
1 Tablespoon	green peppercorns
15 cloves	garlic, peeled
2 quarts	goat's milk
1	crotin chevignol (goat's cheese), approximately 3 ounces
1 Tablespoon	parsley
3 teaspoons	sour cream

Cut leek whites off in one piece and slice green thinly. Rub pork loin with peppercorn and brown on all sides in a deep (6-inch) casserole or dutch oven. Remove from pan and add garlic cloves. Cook until light gold and remove from pan. Add green leeks and steam for 5 minutes. Put meat and garlic back into casserole and cover with goats milk. Cover and cook in 325° oven for 1½ hours until meat is tender. Remove pork to warm platter, lift out garlic cloves and reduce milk in pan to ⅓.

Cook leek whites. Let cool and remove center third of each piece, leaving a cylinder to be filled. In small bowl, mash the cooked garlic with the softened goat cheese and fresh chopped parsley and 1 teaspoon sour cream. Stuff leeks with this mixture. Place leeks in oven until just warm. Slice pork loin. Strain milk and whisk in 2 teaspoons sour cream. Season to taste and serve. **Serves:** 6-8

Jarrets de Veal Tout Paris

Submitted by Chef Daniel Bonnot

½ cup	flour
2½ pounds	shank bone of veal, saw into 2-inch pieces
⅓ cup	olive oil
1 teaspoon	butter
2	carrots, finely sliced
1	onion, finely sliced
1 branch	celery, finely sliced
2	tomatoes, skinned, seeded, diced
1 teaspoon	tomato paste
1 cup	white wine
1 cup	stock (enough to come at least ⅓ up the bone)
1	bay leaf
1 pinch	thyme
	salt and pepper
3 ounces	crawfish tails
1 teaspoon	chopped parsley
	zest of ½ orange and ½ lemon
4 sliced	truffles

Flour both sides of veal, pour olive oil in a heavy casserole, brown meat on both sides, remove meat, pour off fat and add butter with finely sliced vegetables. Cook vegetables all together for a few minutes and add the fresh tomatoes and tomato paste to casserole and mix for a few minutes. Deglaze casserole with wine and veal stock, replace meat in the casserole, add bay leaf, thyme, salt and pepper. Simmer covered.

After veal has cooked about 1½ hours (when tender) skim off fat, remove from the casserole, and place meat where it will remain hot. Reduce sauce, add crawfish tails, chopped parsley, and zest of orange and lemon, pour sauce over the veal and place each slice of truffles over bones. Serve with fresh noodles on the side. **Serves:** 4

The Floating Palace

Courtesy of Riverwalk

One of the wonders of the era before the Civil War was the Floating Palace, a waterborne circus that travelled the Mississippi River system. Almost two hundred feet long and thirty-five feet wide, it was too large to propel itself. The Palace could accomodate 3,400 persons around its arena, where "the largest collection of beasts and desert monsters" were displayed; including lions, an elephant, a rhinoceros, a hippopotamus, and rare birds. The Palace was towed by a sidewheel steamboat, on which plays, concerts, and vaudeville acts were presented. The whole thing was so brilliantly lit by acetylene gas that many spectators found the illumination as exciting as the entertainment. The Palace issued its own daily newspaper, edited and printed on board, and carried a staff of almost one hundred. In 1862, it was taken over by the Confederacy for a hospital stationed in New Orleans.

Elephant Stew

Submitted by Mary Michael

No cookbook is complete without this one.

1 medium	**elephant**
2	**rabbits (optional)**
	salt and pepper to taste
	brown gravy (lots!)

Cut elephant into bite size pieces. This will take about 2 months. Reserve the trunk—you will need something to put the pieces in. Add enough brown gravy to cover. Cook on kerosene stove for about 4 weeks at 465°.

Hint: This will serve 3,800 people. If more are expected, the 2 rabbits may be added. Do this only if necessary—as most people do not like to find "hare" in their stew!

Tripe Stew

Submitted by Alcée-Hymel Family

2 pounds	tripe
¼ cup	oil
¼ cup	flour
½ cup	celery, finely chopped
½ cup	onions, finely chopped
1	bell pepper cut into thin strips
1 bunch	green onions (bottoms and tops)
1 can (16 ounces)	tomatoes, chopped
pinch	of sugar
sprig	of thyme
1	bay leaf
3 or 4 cloves	garlic, minced
	water
	parsley
	salt
	Tabasco® or cayenne pepper to taste

Wash tripe well, put in pot with water, bring to boil, take out and scrape. Cut into strips (desired size). Set aside.

Make roux with oil and flour until golden brown. Add celery, onions, bell pepper, bottoms only of green onions (save tops for later use) and sauté until tender. Add tomatoes and sauté for 10 minutes. Add pinch of sugar. Add sprig of thyme, bay leaf, green onion tops and garlic. Add cut up tripe and sauté for 10 minutes, stirring frequently. Add water, parsley, salt, Tabasco or cayenne pepper to taste, and cook until tripe is tender. Serve over rice or mashed potatoes. **Serves: 8**

Looking Back

Courtesy of Riverwalk

During the mid-1800s, the steamboat lines competed fiercely for limited passengers and often participated in dangerous races to reach their destinations in the shortest time possible. This intense competition often led to riverboat rivalries, as pilots raced to enchance their prestige and increase their passenger list.

The most renowned rivalry was probably that which existed between the Natchez's Captain, Thomas P. Leathers and Captain John Cannon of the Robert E. Lee. The Natchez was generally considered to be the swiftest "packet," as they were called, after breaking the record for the New Orleans to St. Louis run by 1 hour and 12 minutes. The previous record for the race was 11 days and had been shortened by the Natchez to approximately 4 days.

As fate would have it, on June 30, 1870, the Natchez and the Robert E. Lee were both scheduled to make the New Orleans-St. Louis run. When the cannon was fired to begin the departure, the Robert E. Lee edged a 3 minute and 45 second headstart which it kept throughout the race. The Robert E. Lee arrived in St. Louis in a remarkable 3 days, 18 hours and 14 minutes time, setting an amazing new record.

The race tradition is still going strong in New Orleans, as can be witnessed each year when the riverboats Delta Queen and Natchez take their marks to run from Audubon Landing downriver to Algiers Point. The annual race begins the opening of the spring French Quarter Festival and draws enthusiastic crowds along both banks of the Mississippi River.

Mississippi Pilot Salad

Submitted by Terry Newkirk, Executive Chef, Kabby's New Orleans Hilton Seafood Restaurant

1 pound	chopped lettuce
12	boiled shrimp, peeled and deveined
1 pound	steamed redfish fillet
2 cups	crawfish tail meat
12	steamed oysters cherry tomatoes, lemons, radish, green onion and black olives for garnish

Place bed of lettuce on plate. Arrange seafood on top, and add garnish. Serve with desired salad dressing. **Yield:** 4 salads

Bootlegger

Submitted by Carolyn Casey

My grandfather has been dead since 1959 and was 83 years old when he died. During prohibition he was a bootlegger and would make gin or whiskey and would put it in the upstairs bathroom in the bathtub. His brother was the assessor and would know when the raids were going to be made. When they were coming out for a raid, my grandfather would send one of his daughters up into the bathroom. If they were really going to come to look into the house, they would say his daughter was bathing because nobody would enter the bathroom if a girl was bathing. That way they never caught him.

Thanks to the repeal of prohibition, the following recipes are enhanced by the use of "spirits" in one form or another.

Baby Veal "Christian"

Submitted by Christian's Restaurant

12 (3 ounces each)	baby veal cutlets
	salt and pepper
	(freshly ground)
	flour
¾ stick	butter
⅓ cup	ruby port wine
3 cups	whipping cream
6 ounces	morel mushrooms
	(canned or reconsti-
	tuted from dried)

Salt and pepper cutlets and sprinkle with flour. Melt butter in skillet and lightly brown cutlets on both sides making sure not to overcook. Remove cutlets from skillet and place on side to keep warm. Remove excess butter from skillet and add the port wine. On a high fire, reduce liquid by half, add cream and the morel mushrooms. Reduce the sauce and season with salt and pepper. Spoon sauce over cutlets and serve immediately.

Note: Morel mushrooms usually come from Switzerland and can be obtained canned or dried. If the dried version is obtained, soak the mushrooms overnight and clean them well. Drain well of all liquid before using for cooking. **Serves:** 6

Veal Farcie Versailles

Submitted by Gunter Preuss, The Versailles Restaurant

4 (2 ounces each)	scallopinis of veal
	salt and pepper to
	taste
	lemon juice
	flour
3	beaten eggs
2 Tablespoons	butter
4 Tablespoons	white wine
2 Tablespoons	brown sauce
½ Tablespoon	chopped shallots
4 ounces	crabmeat or shrimp
	mushrooms
	French poupon
	mustard
4 Tablespoons	Half and Half cream
½ teaspoon	flour
2 Tablespoons	melted butter

Sprinkle scallopinis with salt, pepper and lemon juice. Flour scallopinis and drench in whole beaten eggs. Sauté for 1 minute on each side, until done. Drain off fat and add 2 tablespoons white wine and 2 tablespoons brown sauce.

In the meantime sauté shallots and crabmeat in butter with mushrooms and French poupon mustard. After ingredients are sautéed, add 2 tablespoons white wine and Half and Half cream. Thicken seafood stuffing with flour mixed with melted butter.

On preheated plate, place 1 scallopini—ladle seafood stuffing and finish with 3 remaining scallopinis. Cover with preheated brown sauce. **Serves: 4**

Ramos Gin Fizz

Submitted by The Fairmont Hotel (formerly The Roosevelt Hotel)

A local concoction called the Ramos Gin Fizz (named after Henry Ramos) was invented for people like Miss Joan Crawford, who after graciously explaining that she didn't drink whiskey, ordered her customary vodka on the rocks. The Ramos Gin Fizz was such a favorite of late, tempestuous Huey Long, that he once ordered a Roosevelt Hotel bartender flown up to New York to mix him one when the bartender in his hotel was unable to concoct one to suit the "Kingfish's" taste.

1 Tablespoon	powdered sugar
3 dashes	lemon juice (½ ounce)
2 dashes	lime juice (¼ ounce)
¼	white of one egg
3 dashes	Orange Flower Water
3 ounces	milk
1¼ ounces	gin
	ice

Combine all ingredients in mixing glass. Shake with metal shaker. Strain in 7 ounce Ramos Glass. **Yield:** 1 Ramos Gin Fizz

Escargot Bourguignonne

Submitted by Gunter Preuss, The Versailles Restaurant

1 cup	red wine
1 Tablespoon	green onions, chopped
½ Tablespoon	shallots, chopped
¼ Tablespoon	garlic, chopped
3 Tablespoons	butter
	salt and pepper to taste
3 cups	brown sauce
36	snails (shells removed)

Combine all ingredients except snails in sauce pan, add snails and cook slowly for 8-10 minutes. Add butter before serving.

Serve in hollowed out round French bread. Heat bread and use top of bread as cover for dish.

Serves: 6

Pecan Sabayon

Submitted by Chef Michel Marcais, La Fete, 1984

3 cups	sugar (granulated)
3 cups	pecan meat
9	egg yolks
1 cup	sugar
½ cup	rum

Caramelize 3 cups sugar in saucepan over direct heat. When sugar starts to brown, add pecans. Stir.

Remove to another pan to cool. When cool, chop sugar/pecan mixture.

Mix egg yolks, 1 cup sugar and rum, whipping until a consistency of a mousse. (This can be done in double boiler over low heat or low fire.)

Blend in pecan mixture and serve. **Serves:** 6

St. Francisville Inn Bread Pudding

Submitted by St. Francisville Inn

1 loaf	bread, stale or not
½ teaspoon	nutmeg
1 teaspoon	cinnamon
1 stick	butter, melted
1 Tablespoon	vanilla
3	eggs, beaten
1½ cups	sugar
1 cup	raisins
3 cups	milk

Rum sauce:

3 Tablespoons	flour
1 cup	of water
1 stick	butter, melted
½ cup	white sugar
1 box (16 ounces)	brown sugar
1 teaspoon	vanilla
½ cup	rum

Tear bread into pieces and mix together with spices, butter, vanilla, sugar, raisins and milk. Put into greased pan and bake at 350° approximately 45 minutes, until custard is soft (not firm). Serve with rum sauce.

For Rum sauce: Blend flour and water together in the blender, then add melted butter. Add white sugar and brown sugar, bring to a boil and stir until thick. When cool, add vanilla and rum. Serve warm over warm pudding. **Serves:** 6

Bread Pudding Soufflé with Whiskey Sauce

Submitted by Commander's Palace Restaurant

Bread pudding:

5	eggs
1 pint	whipping cream
1 cup	sugar
¼ pound	butter
dash	cinnamon
1 Tablespoon	vanilla
¼ cup	raisins
12 1-inch thick slices	fresh or stale French bread (long style loaf)

Soufflé:

	bread pudding
4	egg whites
½ cup	sugar

Whiskey sauce:

1 cup	milk
1 cup	whipping cream
¾ cup	granulated sugar
2½ Tablespoons	cornstarch
2 Tablespoons	bourbon

In a large bowl combine eggs, cream, sugar, butter, cinnamon, vanilla and raisins, mixing well. Pour mixture into a 9-inch square pan, 1¾ inches deep.

Arrange the sliced bread flat in the egg mixture and let stand for 5 minutes to soak up some of the liquid, then turn bread over and let stand for 10 minutes longer. Then push bread down so that most of it is covered by the custard mixture. Do not break the bread.

Set pan into a larger pan filled with water to ½ inch from top. Cover with aluminum foil. Bake in 375° oven for 45 to 50 minutes, uncovering pudding for the last 10 minutes to brown the top. When

243

done, the custard should still be soft, not firm.

For soufflé: (For 2 6-8 ounce ramekins) For every two soufflés use 1½ cups of loosely packed bread pudding. Place into large bowl (stainless steel preferred). Lightly butter and sugar (granulated) the ramekins.

Whip 4 egg whites in another bowl with an electric mixer until they form stiff peaks. Add ½ cup sugar to egg whites and whip for another 15-30 seconds.

Take one spoonful of the whipped egg whites and fold into the bread pudding to moisten, then take the remaining egg whites and fold them in gently. Spoon into the ramekins and mound them up like a dome. Bake in a 350°-375° oven for 25 minutes. Remove and serve immediately with the Bourbon Whiskey sauce.

For Bourbon Whiskey sauce: In a saucepan combine ½ cup of the milk, all of the whipping cream and the sugar, then bring to a simmer.

In a small dish mix the other ½ cup milk and the cornstarch until dissolved, then add to the simmering mixture slowly while whisking. Continue to simmer slowly for 3-5 minutes while stirring. Remove from the stove and stir in the bourbon. **Serves:** 6

Lemon Tequilla Soufflé

Submitted by Versailles Restaurant

⅔ cup	sugar
1 cup	water
6	egg yolks
3 ounces	white wine
2½ ounces	lemon juice
1½ ounces	tequilla
1½ cups	whipped cream

Combine sugar with water in a sauce pan and boil gently until mixture begins to thicken (syrup stage). Remove and let cool thoroughly. When above mixture is cold, combine with the egg yolks, wine, lemon juice and tequilla. Cook this mixture over a low flame, whisking constantly until the foam goes down (taste to be sure eggs are cooked). Place in refrigerator and stir occasionally to cool. When cool, fold in 1½ cups whipped cream and place in freezer.

To serve: Place soufflé in hollowed out lemons, put on a bed of shaved ice and freeze. When about to serve, garnish with whipped cream from a tube, and a mint leaf. **Serves:** 6

Dawn In New Orleans

You sit in a patio in the French Quarter, early one morning when there is no worry or commitment. About 4:30 or 5:00 the sky begins to lighten, and you slowly distinguish the outlines of buildings and treetops against the sky as it turns from black to grey. It is the quietest time of the twenty-four hours. The city is so still, you strain to catch a familiar sound and you realize what they meant— Jelly Roll Morton, Louis Armstrong and the rest— about the way sound used to carry so far in the New Orleans night. And over where Globe Hall used to be, if Buddy Bolden were playing you know you could hear him clearly, along with the people applauding and laughing. You want to go back there, but can't; you can only imagine how it was on a New Orleans morning in 1905.

"Jazz" Milk Punch

Submitted by Gerry Vince

1½ ounces	brandy
¾ ounce	crème de cocoa
2 ounces	milk
1 ounce	Half and Half

Add brandy and liqueur to milk and Half and Half shake. Serve over ice. **Yield:** 1 drink

Oysters Rockefeller

Submitted by Mrs. Richard Leche

My husband was governor of Louisiana from 1936-1939. During his term, Franklin Roosevelt came to New Orleans and we entertained him. FDR loved the Oysters Rockefeller at Antoine's. That is where we took him. My husband kept giving him the oysters off of his plate and after a while began to get worried that he would make the president ill. That was the reason the Mayor Maistre said to President Roosevelt, "How do you like them 'ersters'?"

Oysters Rockefeller

Submitted by Gerri Tusa, Messina's PoBoys, Riverwalk

1 medium	onion, finely chopped
1 rib	celery, finely chopped
3 pounds	chopped spinach
¼ cup	chopped parsley flakes
1 block	butter
2 cups	grated bread crumbs
2-5 drops	Tabasco® sauce
2 teaspoons	anise seed
1 Tablespoon	granulated garlic
1 teaspoon	celery seed
1 teaspoon	salt
1 Tablespoon	Worcestershire sauce
4 Tablespoons	grated romano cheese
5 dozen medium-sized	raw oysters

Cook and stir onion and celery until tender. Add other ingredients except oysters and cook 5 minutes. Spoon 1 tablespoon of mixture over raw oyster on clean shell. Bake at 350° for 35-40 minutes. **Yield:** 5 dozen

Noni's Oysters Rockefeller

Submitted by Chiqui Collier, Cookery N'Orleans Style Restaurant

1 pound	fresh spinach, cooked, drained and chopped
4	green onions with tops, chopped
2 ribs	celery with leaves, chopped
8 sprigs	parsley (leaves only)
dash	Tabasco®
6	anchovy fillets or equal amount of paste
1½ Tablespoons	Lea & Perrins Worcestershire®
6-8 Tablespoons	Anisette liqueur (or more to taste)
2 sticks	melted butter parmesan cheese
¾ cup	seasoned bread crumbs
4 dozen	oysters

Blend all ingredients except cheese, bread crumbs, and oysters in processor or blender until thoroughly puréed. Stir in bread crumbs to make a slightly moist dressing. Broil drained fresh oysters on the half shell* until edges curl (or sauté in a little butter until edges curl and place in a scallop shell or a ramekin). Cover each oyster with sauce and sprinkle with cheese. Broil 10 minutes.

*Place scrubbed oyster shells in a pie plate filled with rock salt. **Serves: 8**

Oysters Peacock

Submitted by Executive Chef John Carey, The Windsor Court Hotel

½	red bell pepper
½	green bell pepper
1	leek
3	shallots
¼ pound	Shitake mushrooms
1 teaspoon	fresh thyme
1 teaspoon	fresh marjoram
3 teaspoons	salt
2 teaspoons	cayenne pepper
2 teaspoons	white pepper
2 teaspoons	black pepper
1 teaspoon	chili powder
1 teaspoon	paprika pepper
16 ounces	butter
2 cups	bread crumbs
16	fresh oysters in their shells and their juice
4-6 ounces	angel hair pasta
	diced tomatoes

Chop fine, bell peppers, leek, shallots, mushrooms, thyme and marjoram, salt, and spices, and sauté in 4 ounces of the butter until cooked through. Allow this mixture to cool.

In a mixing bowl combine the rest of the butter, the cooled mixture of chopped ingredients and the bread crumbs, and mix until smooth.

Make patties the size of an oyster shell, approximately ½-inch thick, and place patties on top of each oyster and shell.

Cook 10 minutes at 400°.

Serve with angel hair pasta cooked al dente, and fresh diced tomatoes. **Serves:** 4, as an appetizer

Cream of Oysters Rockefeller Soup

Submitted by Chef Frank Brigtsen, Brigtsen's Restaurant

Brigtsen's Restaurant is still considered a new restaurant by New Orleans' standards. It opened in March 1985, but owner, Chef Frank Brigtsen is already winning awards for his culinary talent. Frank, his wife, and her sister were formerly with K-Paul's Restaurant where Frank "cooked Cajun." Brigtsen's features Creole cuisine which is Frank's first love—and it shows!

5 cups	oyster liquor (the liquid that comes with shucked oysters)
3 quarts	heavy whipping cream (40% butterfat)
1 pound	sweet unsalted butter
4 cups	diced yellow onions (¼ inch)
5 cups	diced ribs of celery (¼ inch)
6 cups	coarsely chopped spinach (all stems removed)
8 cups	sliced green onions (white and green sections)
1½ teaspoons	finely minced garlic
2½ cups	finely chopped parsley (flat parsley preferred)
3 Tablespoons	Chef Paul Prudhomme's Seafood Magic Seasoning®

1 Tablespoon plus	
1 teaspoon	salt
2 Tablespoons	white all-purpose flour
1¾ cups	Herbsaint® (an Anise-flavored liqueur made in New Orleans)
	cayenne pepper
40 medium or 60 small	shucked oysters

In a 2 quart saucepan bring oyster liquor to a boil; turn down heat and keep warm.

In a 5 quart saucepan bring the whipping cream to a boil; turn down heat and keep warm.

In a 10 quart saucepan melt butter over medium-high heat. Add onions, celery, spinach, green onions, garlic, parsley, seafood seasoning and salt. Cook these ingredients until soft, about 10 minutes.

Lower heat to medium and add flour. Cook about 4 to 5 minutes, stirring constantly. Let mixture stick to bottom of pan, scraping and stirring constantly.

Add the warm oyster liquor, the Herbsaint and let cook 20 minutes more, scraping and stirring constantly.

Remove vegetable mixture from stove and purée. Return to saucepan and bring back to a boil. Add the warm cream and let simmer 40-45 minutes. Correct seasoning with salt and red pepper (preferably cayenne).

To serve, poach 2 medium or 3 small oysters per serving in their liquor and cover with 4-5 ounces of soup base. Serve in preheated 8 ounce soup or bouillon cups. **Yield:** 20 tasting size portions.

Oysters A La Olivier

Submitted by The Honorable Lindy (Mrs. Hale) Boggs, M.C.

1 Tablespoon	green onions
½ teaspoon	garlic
1 can (8 ounces)	mushrooms
2 dozen	large oysters
	flour
1½ sticks	butter
½ teaspoon	salt
½ teaspoon	black pepper
6-8 ounces	dry sherry
1 Tablespoon	Worcestershire sauce
6 slices	buttered toast
2 Tablespoons	chopped parsley

Chop together green onions, garlic and mushrooms. Dry the oysters and powder with flour. In heavy frying pan, heat ½ stick butter until bubbly. Quickly brown oysters in the butter until edges curl. Remove from heat. In another pan, place chopped green onions, garlic and mushrooms. Add 1 stick of butter and fry until melted. Add salt and pepper, sherry and Worcestershire sauce. Stir until blended. Place oysters on buttered toast, pour sauce over oysters and garnish with chopped parsley. **Serves:** 4-6

Memère's Oyster Patties

Submitted by Pat McDonald Gomez, Aunt Sally's Praline Shop

Our dear grandmother, Diane Jacquet Bagur, helped open Aunt Sally's Praline Shops with her husband, Pierre E. Bagur, Sr., in the early 1930s. She was a very fine Creole cook and in her later years became an accomplished artist. Born into an old New Orleans Creole family, Memère learned early how to prepare traditional Creole dishes. She had a perfect understanding of the subtle seasonings and sauces that are a mainstay in New Orleans' Creole cuisine. Although today's Creole cooking has become infused with Italian and African influences, Memère's method of cooking was of pure French and Spanish descent. Her dishes were never hot, spicy or overly rich—just perfectly sublime and delicious. One of our favorite dishes was one that she saved for special occasions, her oyster patties. They were so popular that she would have to make sure that none of us would "snitch" a few before they were placed on the silver serving platter. Memère died at the age of 98 in 1986, but she left with us a deep appreciation for fine food, and a unique culinary heritage.

Memère's Oyster Patties

Submitted by Pat McDonald Gomez, Aunt Sally's Praline Shop

½ cup	cooking oil
2 Tablespoons	flour
1 bunch	green onions, chopped
1 pod	garlic, minced
½ bunch	parsley, minced
1	green pepper, chopped
½	yellow onion, chopped
3 dozen	oysters
	oyster water
	bay leaf
	cayenne
	salt
	pepper
36	puff pastry shells

Place oil in deep iron skillet. When oil is hot, slowly add flour and stir until mixture becomes a smooth paste. Allow roux to brown to a deep caramel color. Add chopped vegetables to roux, and allow to cook until vegetables are transparent and wilted. Do not allow mixture to burn. Meanwhile drain oysters in a sieve, reserving oyster water. Pick oysters for bits of shell. Slowly add oyster water to vegetables and roux mixture, stirring all the time to make a thick sauce. Do not make sauce too watery, because oysters will add more liquid to sauce. Add bay leaf, cayenne, salt and pepper to taste. Allow sauce to cook for 10 minutes at a low simmer. Add oysters and continue simmering on low fire until oysters curl. If mixture is too thick, add water and return to boil.

Remove tops for puff pastry patties. Fill cocktail size pattyshells with an oyster and sauce, and place in 350° oven until the patty shells have thoroughly warmed. If any sauce is left over, it can be used as a base for gumbo or soup, or delicious for dipping slices of crisp French bread. **Serves: 6**

Sundays Before the Superdome

Submitted by Chiqui Collier, Cookery N'Orleans Style Restaurant

There was a very famous Italian Restaurant that my Grandfather took my father to as a child. My father also took us there every Easter for dinner. It was a family owned business. They had the same waiters as they had in my father's youth. Harold was our favorite, but my mother made friends with one named Freddie who spoke Spanish like she did.

After several flirtatious visits, my mother persuaded him to reveal the restaurant's fabulous recipe for "Artichokes Stuffed with Veal." It's always been a family favorite. The restaurant is gone now; its original location is part of the Louisiana Superdome. I'll never forget our Sunday dinners there, and every Spring when artichokes are in season, you can still find these around our house.

Artichokes Stuffed with Veal

Submitted by Chiqui Collier, Cookery N'Orleans Style Restaurant

#I

1 large	French bread, soaked in water, squeezed dry and finely chopped
½ teaspoon	salt
¼ teaspoon	lemon pepper
1 cup	pine nuts
1 Tablespoon	Guava jelly (not paste)
	olive oil

#II

½ pound	ground baby veal
½ pound	ground round steak
1 medium	onion, chopped
2 large toes	garlic, minced
	salt to taste
	lemon pepper to taste
	olive oil
½ cup	grated parmesan or romano cheese

#III

3	artichokes, cleaned, trimmed
	juice of 1 lemon
	olive oil
1	lemon, sliced
1 quart	fresh chicken stock

Cook all ingredients in #I in a heavy skillet using a little olive oil. Cook over low flame until it stops "steaming." Cool. In separate skillet heat olive oil and add all ingredients (except cheese) in #II until lightly browned. Combine with bread mixture adding cheese. Boil the artichokes in water with lemon juice for 10 minutes; drain. Divide bread dressing evenly between the three artichokes. Place in a 5 quart Dutch oven. Drizzle with olive oil and top with sliced lemon. Fill the pot 1½" deep with the chicken stock and cover. Steam on low flame 2½ to 3 hours. Uncover and run under broiler to brown. **Note:** Make NO substitutions! **Serves:** 3

Plantation Pralines

Courtesy of Riverwalk

He was an elderly Creole known as Chevalier, never seen without his dog and monkey, his constant companions. He hated the Americans who now occupied Louisiana. He didn't like change at all, like the concept of equality that many Creoles believed in after the French Revolution. Poppycock! He was even more shocked by the popular dress of the period, pantaloons and appearing in public without a wig! Until the day he died, he wore the outmoded powdered wig and queue, knee breeches, silk stockings, frizzled cuffs and shirt front, and silver buckles on his slippers. Because he had squandered most of his money on schemes to liberate Louisiana from the Americans, he opened a candy and bake shop on Chartres near Dumaine. There he sold a plantation delicacy called praline; the first time that confection was ever offered for sale in New Orleans.

Pecan Pralines

Submitted by The Alcée-Hymel Family

1 cup	brown sugar
1 cup	white sugar
½ cup	evaporated milk
2 Tablespoons	butter
1 cup	pecan halves
¼ teaspoon	pure vanilla

Combine the sugar and milk and bring to a boil, stirring occasionally. Add the butter, pecans and vanilla and cook until the syrup reaches the "soft ball stage," 238°. Cool without disturbing until somewhat thickened, but not until it loses its gloss. Drop by tablespoons onto a well greased, flat surface. (A piece of marble is best for this.) The candy will flatten out into large pralines.

Yield: approximately 24

257

Aunt Sally's Praline Sauce

Submitted by Pat McDonald Gomez, Aunt Sally's Praline Shop

The recipe for Aunt Sally's original Creole pralines is a closely guarded family secret, but we do share our secret for a special family treat. For holidays or birthday dinners, we will often make a praline sauce to pour over vanilla ice cream. It's important that the ice cream be of the rich, intense vanilla flavored—a good homemade ice cream with real vanilla is ideal. The creamy texture of the ice cream is a superb match for the crunchy sweet flavor of the sauce.

6	**Aunt Sally's Original Creole Pralines®**
	water or evaporated milk
8 scoops	**vanilla ice cream**

Place the pralines in the top section of a double boiler and place the pan over boiling water. Add just enough water or milk to the melting candy so that the mixture is not too thick or dry. Pour the sauce warm over ice cream. C'est bon! **Serves:** 4

Praline Frosting

Submitted Shirley Childress

¼ cup	**butter flavored Crisco®**
½ cup	**chopped pecans**
¼ cup	**milk**
½ teaspoon	**vanilla**
3-3½ cups	**powdered sugar**

In small saucepan combine Crisco and pecans. Cook over medium heat until Crisco melts. Remove from heat. Blend in milk and vanilla. Transfer to medium mixing bowl. Add powdered sugar, 1 cup at a time, beating at medium speed of electric mixer until frosting is of desired consistency. Spread on cooled cake. **Yield:** enough icing for 1 cake

Moving Day

Submitted by Emily Halley
(daughter of a former President of Tulane)

In New Orleans, October 1st was the day to move. I'm not really sure why! I suppose it was because your winter clothes were still packed, and it was cool enough after the long hot summers.

"Welcome" Eggplant Casserole

Submitted by Mrs. Clarence C. Clifton

1½ pounds	eggplant
2 Tablespoons	shortening
1 large	onion, chopped
2 Tablespoons each:	parsley (chopped), thyme (chopped), paprika, pepper, salt
1 pound	cooked shrimp
2 slices	bread
	bread crumbs

To prevent bitter eggplant dishes, boil the whole unpared eggplant until tender. Let cool, peel and remove the bitter seeds and their sacks which come out whole. Heat shortening in heavy skillet, glaze the onions, add the well-drained eggplant, parsley, seasonings. Let simmer, then add cooked shrimp and the bread, which has been almost dissolved in water. Mix well and simmer again. Turn into greased casserole; top with crumbs. Bake at 350° for twenty or thirty minutes. **Serves:** 4

The Judge Presides Over the Stove

Submitted by Mercedes Andrus

My late husband, Alex, loved to cook and did for many a dinner party. He was a real gourmet and every item he made was marvelous, but he demanded a lot of assistance. It was "please chop the onions" and "now hand me a spoon."

Finally I realized that he didn't cook, he presided over the stove. He was a judge and just as officious in the kitchen as on the bench. The following recipe was one of our favorites and one of his best.

Eggplant and Shrimp

Submitted by Mercedes Andrus (Judge Alexander Andrus)

2 large	eggplants
1	onion
1	bell pepper
3 stems	celery
	olive oil
1½ pounds	shrimp, raw and peeled and cut into 2 or 3 pieces each salt, red and black pepper Italian style bread crumbs

Peel and dice eggplants (about 1 cubic inch) and boil in seasoned water until tender (use aluminum pot), drain in colander and set aside. Place finely chopped vegetables in iron pot with olive oil and simmer on low fire until wilted. Add raw shrimp and cook on low fire for 10 to 12 minutes. Blend cooked vegetables and shrimp into cooked eggplants adding seasoning to taste and adding bread crumbs for proper consistency. Place in casserole and sprinkle top with bread crumbs. Heat in 350° oven before serving. **Serves: 8**

Sunflower Salad

Submitted by Mercedes Andrus (Judge Alexander Andrus)

2 bottles (6½ ounces each)	hearts of artichokes
1 small can (6 ounces)	diced (or cut) beets
2 cans (8 ounces each)	green asparagus tips
1	avocado, cut lengthwise into thin slices
1 large	bell pepper, cut lengthwise into thin slices
1	tomato cut into small wedges
1 or 2	pimentos
	salad dressing
1 large	oval plate (18 inches in diameter)

In central portion of oval plate, form circular levee with hearts of artichokes leaving 3-inch diameter center. Fill center with diced beets. Alternate asparagus tips, sliced avocado and sliced bell pepper on outer perimeter of levee and perpendicular thereto so vegetables form spokes of wheel around center. Place tomato wedges (skin up) every 2 or 3 inches within vegetables. Form circle with thin slices of pimentos on outer edge. Add salad dressing of choice. **Serves: 8**

Chapter VI
Lagniappe
The Making of a Legend

The rest of this book is "Lagniappe." It is a part of New Orleans history being formed—A Legend in the Making.

Lagniappe

Submitted by Dee Simon

When you used to go to the corner grocery store you would ask for things like "a piece of pickle meat for 50 cents" or "a nickel's worth of red beans and a nickel's worth of rice." They would scoop out the amount from big tubs. If you bought your red beans and rice they would throw in the seasoning as lagniappe. New Orleanians love to get lagniappe (just a little something extra).

Developing the Riverfront's "Golden Mile" (Anchored by Rouse's Riverwalk)

Courtesy of Port of New Orleans
Excerpts from the article by Russ Greenbaum

They are starting to call it the riverfront's "Golden Mile." It starts at the Spanish Plaza at the foot of Canal Street and extends upriver to where the new Mississippi River Bridge arches over land just past the New Orleans Convention Center.

What is obvious is that the remarkable changes that have taken place have had a profound effect on the image and activities of the downtown riverfront. It was there that not too long ago, bags of coffee and bales of cotton were hustled in and out of crowded transit sheds by gangs of stevedores, while cargo vessels lined the wharves. Those vessels have been replaced by sleek modern cruise ships and harbor tour boats like The Creole Queen and shops and restaurants at the "Riverwalk" specialty marketplace.

The Rouse Company's Riverwalk, New Orleans'

own riverfront marketplace, is a collection of unique merchants gathered along the banks of the Mississippi River. Open since the summer of 1986, it has unusual retail shops, pushcarts and kiosks selling creative merchandise, and a food experience from gourmet specialty fast food to cafés and restaurants with magnificent views of the water.

Lester E. Kabacoff, more than any other individual, is responsible for the radical changes in this downtown riverfront. The rejuvenation began in the early 1970s with the development of the 30-story Hilton Hotel at the foot of Poydras Street. This was the first high-rise building close to and overlooking the river since the completion of the International Trade Mart (now the World Trade Center) in 1967.

In conjunction with the development of the hotel, Kabacoff cast his eye on the Lower Poydras Wharf as a place for a shopping and restaurant complex connected to the hotel by two enclosed walkways over the tracks. In this respect his idea predated Rouse's Riverwalk by a decade. Discussions with the Port led to the plan of converting the wharf into a cruise passenger terminal that included the shopping mall, which would serve to enhance passenger operations. This met the requirement that any use of the wharf had to have a maritime connection. The connecting walkways provided convenient access to the terminal and to lodging for passengers at the hotel.

The passenger terminal was completed even before the Hilton Hotel opened its doors in 1977. It has proved to be a decided asset and is regularly used by cruise ships, such as those operated by the Royal Viking Line, the Royal Caribbean Line and the Costa Line, which make regular calls at New Orleans.

The 1,600-room hotel, the New Orleans Convention Center, and Riverwalk, have all helped to create an exciting "happening" on the Golden Mile—certainly a "legend in the making."

Crawfish Étouffée

Submitted by Terry Newkirk, Executive Chef, Kabby's
The New Orleans Hilton Seafood Restaurant

1 medium	bell pepper, chopped
1 medium	onion, chopped
2 ounces	butter
2 cloves	garlic, chopped
20 ounces	crawfish tail meat with fat
2 ounces	flour
1 pint	shellfish stock or water
	salt
	black pepper
	cayenne pepper
	Kitchen Bouquet® (optional)
16 ounces	cooked rice
2 Tablespoons	green onions, chopped

Sauté bell pepper and onion in butter until tender. Add garlic and crawfish tails. Cook 2 minutes. Add flour and cook until slightly browned. Add stock, simmer 10 minutes. If water is used, simmer 20-30 minutes. Season with salt and pepper. Kitchen Bouquet can be added to darken if needed. Serve over rice. Garnish with chopped green onions. **Serves:** 4

Red Beans and Rice With Smoked Sausage

Submitted by Terry Newkirk, Executive Chef, Kabby's
The New Orleans Hilton Seafood Restaurant

½ cup	bell pepper, chopped
½ cup	onions, chopped
½ cup	celery, chopped
¼ cup	bacon fat
2	bay leaves
1 Tablespoon	garlic, chopped
2	fresh ham hocks
½ pound	pickled pork
1 pound	dried red kidney beans
1 gallon	water
	salt and pepper to taste
	smoked sausage, 6 ounces per portion
	steamed rice, 4 ounces per portion

Sauté vegetables in bacon fat until tender. Add spices, ham hocks, pickled pork and dried beans. Sauté until skin on beans wrinkles. Add water, simmer until beans are very soft and liquid is creamy. Add more water if needed. Adjust seasoning with salt and pepper. Broil sausage. Serve beans over steamed rice with sausage on the side.

Serves: 4 or more

Windsor Court Hotel and Grill Room

The Windsor Court Hotel, located just a few short blocks from the waterfront is, after only two years in existence, a member of the "Leading Hotels of the World." It is renowned for quality service, and a stunning decor which encompasses an art collection valued at $4 million.

"Afternoon Tea," which has become an event, happens here every day from 2:00 until 6:00 p.m. and is presented in the British fashion. Loose tea is poured through a strainer (many varieties are available) and is served with three courses. First, there is a selection of delicious finger sandwiches, then black currant scones accompanied by lemon curd, raspberry preserves, sweet butter and Devonshire cream. Lastly, sweets are presented—chocolate dipped strawberries, chocolate truffles and assorted cookies.

Following are recipes for scones, lemon tart, and the "proper" way to make tea.

English Tea

Submitted by the Windsor Court Hotel

Boil water; pour into silver tea pot with loose tea leaves and brew. Strain and pour into china cup. Serve with scones.

Scones

Submitted by the Windsor Court Hotel

2½ cups	all-purpose flour
5 teaspoons	double-acting baking powder
4 teaspoons	sugar
⅛ teaspoon	salt
¾ stick	cold, unsalted butter, cut into bits
¾ cup	heavy cream
2 large	eggs
¾ cup	dried currants
	egg wash made by beating 1 egg with
⅓ cup	milk
1 Tablespoon	sugar

In a bowl sift together the flour, the baking powder, 4 teaspoons of the sugar, and the salt; add the butter, and blend the mixture until it resembles meal. Stir in the cream, the eggs, and the currants, and combine the mixture until it just forms a dough.

Pat out the dough 1-inch thick on a floured surface, and with a floured 2-inch cutter cut it into rounds, and arrange the scones on a buttered baking sheet. Brush the tops of the scones with the egg wash, sprinkle the scones with the 1 tablespoon sugar, and bake them in a preheated 450° oven until golden brown. **Yield:** approximately 12

Lemon Tart

Submitted by The Windsor Court Hotel

5	eggs
5	egg yolks
10 ounces	sugar
5	lemons (juice of all 5, zest of 2)
3 ounces	clarified butter, melted (unsalted)
1 11-inch	pre-baked tart shell

Place eggs, yolks, sugar, and lemon ingredients in a large mixing bowl. In a large brazier on top of stove, boil water filled halfway up. (The greater the area of the bowl which you can heat, the more evenly the entire mixture will cook.)

Whip the mixture quickly (as if making hollandaise). Do not stop whipping until you can draw the whip through the mixture and it forms a ridge which stays in place.

At this point, take from the heat and whip in butter. Pour into prebaked tart shell, and brown underneath broiler.

Refrigerate and serve with raspberry sauce.

Raspberry Sauce:

2 pints	fresh raspberries
2 Tablespoons	clover honey
2 teaspoons	sugar (or to taste, depending on sweetness of berries)
	juice of half lime

Pass fresh berries through a fine sieve, which will result in juice. Get rid of seeds. Add other ingredients to juice in a bowl, mix, and serve over the Lemon Tart. (This may be made ahead of time and refrigerated.) **Yield:** 1 tart with sauce

Café Colada

Submitted by Michael Fabian

2 ounces	rum
2 ounces	Crème de Cocoa
4 ounces	Cream of Coconut
2 cups	cold coffee or espresso (the stronger the better)
2 cups	ice
½ teaspoon	vanilla
2 ounces	heavy cream

Place all ingredients in blender. Blend on high speed until frappéd. Serve in stemmed water goblet. Garnish with whipped cream and cherry if desired. (For more coffee flavor, use ice that has been made from cold coffee). **Serves:** 4

Café Milano

Submitted by Michael Fabian

4 ounces	Grande Marnier® liqueur
2 ounces	Kahlua®
3 cups	hot coffee
	sugar (if desired)
	whipped cream
	shaved chocolate

Mix first three ingredients. Sweeten to taste. Top with whipped cream and chocolate. **Serves:** 4

Make Groceries

Submitted by Jeanne Roslyn Lemmon

Only in New Orleans do people say they "make groceries." In any other city this phrase would make no sense. New Orleanians have translated the French phrase "faire le marcher" literally—make the market, to making groceries. So the next time someone says that they have to make groceries, you will know what they mean!

Whole Food Company Chicken Salad

Submitted by Peter Roy

The Whole Food Company, now located in Riverwalk as well as on Esplanade Avenue, has won its place as the most successful natural food grocery store in town.

This chicken salad is made on a daily basis. It is by far the best selling salad that is offered and the secret of its taste lies in the quality ingredients and in the freshness of its preparation.

2-3 pounds	cooked natural chicken breast
½ cup	celery
½ cup	chopped green onions
¾ cup	Westbrae Natural Mayonnaise®
1 Tablespoon	Zatarain's Creole Mustard®
2 teaspoons	Vegesal® (vegetable salt seasoning)
1 teaspoon	white pepper
½ teaspoon	Tabasco®

Cooked chicken should be chopped into large chunks, approximately one-inch dice. Add chopped celery and onions to chicken mixture. Mix mayonnaise and mustard, Vegesal, white pepper, and Tabasco, and add to chicken. Blend together all ingredients, gently. Correct seasonings. This chicken salad is chunky and best when a bit spicy.

Yield: 3 quarts

Funnel Cakes

Submitted by Norman and Elaine Barrios

Like New Orleans beignets, funnel cakes are fried doughnuts, but in quite a different shape. The batter is made from 7 ingredients using a special soft wheat flour. They are cooked in a very high grade soy bean oil at 350°. Stainless steel rings are placed inside a doughnut frýer and the batter is poured into a regular household funnel. The funnel is then held over the rings above the oil and as the batter pours out of the funnel, it creates small loops and curlicues. This allows the batter to cook on all sides, which produces the crunch.

Fish Supreme

Submitted by Norman and Elaine Barrios

8-12	fish fillets
	salt and pepper to taste
¼ pound	butter
3-5	mushrooms, sliced paper thin
½ medium	onion, sliced paper thin
¼	bell pepper, sliced paper thin
2 toes	garlic, sliced paper thin
1 stalk	celery, sliced paper thin
1½ Tablespoons	flour
2 cups	Chablis
	cream of tartar (optional)
¼ teaspoon	liquid crab boil

Sprinkle fillets with salt and pepper on both sides and place in refrigerator for further use. Melt butter in skillet. Sauté all vegetables in melted butter until celery is wilted. Add flour and incorporate with vegetables. When flour is well incorporated, add wine to create a gravy consistency to your liking. If your gravy is too thin, thicken with some cream of tartar. Allow to simmer for 15 minutes. Add liquid Crab Boil and stir well. Place fish fillets in skillet, being certain all of fish is covered by gravy. Cook until meat is white and flaky, approximately 5-7 minutes. May be served over rice, bread, crackers or whatever. **Serves:** 8-10.

Anthony's Italian Frozia

Submitted by Frankie L. Tusa, Messina's Italian Grocery, Riverwalk

Frozia was Anthony's mother's way of making an Italian omelet. Anthony, who is Frankie's father, thought of applying the Frozia recipe to different seafoods and was very successful.

2½ pounds	finely grated bread crumbs
¾ cup	chopped parsley flakes
¼ cup	whole oregano leaves
⅛ cup	salt
⅛ cup	black pepper
1½ cups	grated Romano cheese
⅓ cup	granulated garlic
3 cups	white flour
3 cups	milk
3	eggs
3 dozen	raw seafood of choice (shrimp, oysters, trout or soft shelled crabs)
1 quart	vegetable oil olive oil to taste

In a bowl, mix bread crumbs, parsley, oregano, salt, pepper, 1 cup cheese and garlic. Put this Frozia mixture in a bowl, put flour in a separate bowl. Add milk and eggs in a third bowl and blend together. Take seafood of choice, coating first in flour, milk and then Frozia mixture and deep fry in vegetable oil until golden brown, drain. Sprinkle with remaining cheese and sprinkle with olive oil to taste. **Serves:** 4-6

Oysters Joseph

Submitted by Gerri Tusa, Messina's Seafood Market, Riverwalk

This dish is served as an entrée in small individual casseroles.

6 dozen	raw oysters, with liquid
2 cups	chopped shallots
1 cup	butter
1 cup	dry white wine
1 teaspoon	salt
2 teaspoons	celery seeds
2 teaspoons	white pepper
1 Tablespoon	granulated garlic
6 Tablespoons	grated Romano cheese
2 cups	bread crumbs
2 cups	Half and Half

Heat oven to 350°. Grease baking dishes. Arrange oysters (with liquid) in baking dishes.

Sauté shallots in butter, about 3 minutes. Add wine, bring to a boil. Add spices, cheese and bread crumbs. Pour half of the Half and Half cream over oysters, spoon bread crumb mixture over oysters. Then pour remaining Half and Half over each individual dish. Heat until bubbly, watching closely, approximately 3 minutes. **Serves: 8**

Redfish Machado

Submitted by Roger Pastore

This delicious redfish dish was created for Pastore's by their chef. It combines local redfish with Italian flavor.

4	**redfish fillets (8 ounces each)**
1 cup	**vegetable oil (for frying)**
	all purpose flour for coating
1 large	**eggplant, sliced**
2	**eggs**
2 Tablespoons	**milk**
	bread crumbs for coating
1 quart	**prepared tomato sauce (your own favorite recipe)**
½ pound	**mozzarella cheese, sliced**

Pan fry fillets in oil about 3 minutes on each side. Set aside. Lightly flour eggplant slices, dip in mixture of egg and milk, then cover with bread crumbs. Fry eggplant until golden brown. Remove. Heat tomato sauce and spoon ½ the sauce into baking dish. Place 4 eggplant slices in dish. On top of eggplant slice place fish, top with another slice of eggplant and mozzarella slices, then cover with remaining sauce. Bake at 350° for 5-8 minutes. **Serves:** 4

Brisas Breeze

Submitted by Joe Pando

This is one of the best tequila drinks we have made. It is semi-sweet and creamy, but the tequila flavor will surely satisfy all tequila drinkers.

2 ounces	tequila
1⅓ ounces	pineapple juice
1⅓ ounces	orange juice
1⅓ ounces	coconut cream
⅓ ounce	grenadine
2 8-ounce cups	filled with crushed ice

Place all ingredients including crushed ice in a blender and blend on medium speed for about 30 seconds, or until a slushy frozen texture is achieved.

Hint: If using ice cubes instead of crushed ice, use less ice and blend on highest speed. If using shaved ice, use more ice and blend on slower speed.

Yield: 2 8-ounce servings.

Creole Delicacies

Submitted by Kenneth Verlander and Lisette Verlander Sutton

Creole Delicacies Company is located at Riverwalk and sells Creole and Cajun specialties such as creamy pecan pralines, rémoulade sauce, hot pepper jelly and Creole seasonings. This recipe comes from owners Kenneth Verlander and his sister Lisette Verlander Sutton and is one of their family favorites.

Herb Chicken

2	fryers, in quarters, washed, dried, trimmed of excess fat
1 Tablespoon	Creole Herb Blend®
½ cup	oil
1 teaspoon	salt
½ teaspoon	pepper
⅛ teaspoon	garlic powder (optional)
	juice 1 lemon
1 can (8 ounces)	chopped mushrooms with liquid
½ cup	sherry or white wine (optional)
½ cup	chopped parsley

Mix Creole Herb Blend, oil, salt, pepper, garlic powder and lemon. Rub mixture well into chicken. Put chicken in baking pan, skin side up. Bake at 450° for 10 minutes, lower temperature to 350° for 15 minutes. Add mushrooms, sherry or wine and parsley. Cook 20 minutes longer until well done.

Note: Creole Herb Blend is made by Creole Delicacies Kitchens, Incorporated. It is a mixture of thyme, bay leaf and marjoram. **Serves:** 6-8

Dictionary of Terms
(for out-of-towners)

The terms Cajun and Creole are sometimes used interchangeably to describe Louisiana food and its legendry. Although there is some overlap in cultures, they are two distinctly separate entities.

Cajuns are the country cousins of the Creoles and are descendants of the French that lived along the coast of Nova Scotia or Acadia. They settled in Louisiana after fleeing religious persecution and drifting for many years. Their cooking is prepared with fresh local ingredients, highly seasoned, often from a steaming cast-iron pot that has been simmering for hours. Their philosophy: "There is always room for more."

The Creoles are descendants of the early French and Spanish settlers of New Orleans. Their cooking style has been influenced by the cultures of the Africans, the American Indians, the people from the Caribbean as well as the Italians, Germans, Irish, English and Yugoslavians who later came to Louisiana. The food they prepare is an urban cuisine, rich with tomatoes, herbs and spices and is elegantly served in separate courses, each in its own sauce.

1. **Andouille (an-dó-ee)** A very popular Cajun sausage made from pure pork.

2. **Banquette (bank-ette)** A sidewalk in New Orleans.

3. **Barbecued Shrimp** Don't let the name fool you. This famous local dish is delicious, but not barbecued at all. It is, in fact, served in a peppery "hot" butter sauce, in its own shell, with the head still on.

4. **Beignets (ben-yaýs)** Also called French Market Doughnuts. Yeast doughnuts cut into rectangles, deep fried and served hot with powdered sugar (preferably with some strong New Orleans coffee).

5. **Café au Lait (cafay-ó-lay)** Strong chicory coffee poured together with hot milk.

6. **Chicory** A ground root which is mixed with coffee before brewing. It makes the coffee strong and adds a bite to it.

7. **Courtbouillon (coo-be-yoń)** Highly seasoned liquid in which to boil crawfish. Often used again in more complex sauces.

8. **Cities of the Dead** Because the ground water is so close to the land surface, tombs must be built above the ground. Local cemeteries look like miniature cities with little streets and fences separating them.

9. **Crawfish (craw-fish)** Nicknamed mudbugs; these are small local edible crustaceans, abundant from December to June. Locals and well-informed visitors never spell or call them crayfish.

10. **Creole Cream Cheese** A milk culture indigenous to New Orleans. It is made like cottage cheese but packed solid with the cream surrounding the curds.

11. **Étouffée (á-too-fay)** A method of cooking where the chicken or shellfish is smothered by chopped vegetables and cooked over a low flame in a tightly covered pan.

12. **Filé (feé-laý)** A powder made from dried sassafras leaves used as a flavoring and a thickening agent in some gumbos.

13. **Gumbo (guḿ-bo)** The word gumbo comes from the African word for okra which the Cajuns learned to use to thicken their delicious soup of the same name. Also found in this dish are shrimp, oysters, crab, sausage, chicken or just vegetables. There are as many variations of gumbos as there are cooks who make them.

14. **Jambalaya (jom-ba-lié-ya)** Derived from the word jambon (French for ham), this dish is a version of the Spanish paella. It is seasoned with chili powder as well

281

as cayenne and the rice is cooked right in with the main ingredients.

15. **Lagniappe (lań-yap)** An old Creole word meaning "a little something extra," like a baker's dozen; buy twelve, get one free.

16. **Mirliton (mer-li-toń)** This vegetable grows on a trellis like vine in New Orleans and is a member of the gourd family. It most resembles squash and is sometimes called chayote, vegetable pear or Christophene.

17. **Muffaletta (moo-fa-lottá)** A special New Orleans sandwich made on an enormous round sesame roll. Inside, are various combinations of thinly sliced meats, cheese, and Italian olive salad.

18. **Piquant (pee-conf)** A term used by Cajuns meaning it's hot and it burns your tongue. Halving the amount of jalapeño peppers makes it less piquant.

19. **Pirogue (peé-ro)** A "one person" flat bottomed Cajun canoe. These boats are built to skim the surface of shallow, slow moving water.

20. **Po-Boy** A sandwich served on long loaves of crisp French bread. Originally very inexpensive and filling which is one explanation for the name. Po-Boys can be made with almost anything inside: roast beef, ham, cheese, shrimp, oysters, and even potatoes.

21. **Praline (praẃ-lene)** A classic Creole candy made with pecans, sugar and sometimes Karo® syrup.

22. **Ramekin (rań-a-kin)** French dish made from bread crumbs, cheese and eggs and served in individual little dishes. Now, the term ramekin sometimes refers to the small dish itself.

23. **Roux (roó)** "First you make a roux," is the often quoted maxim of both Creole and Cajun cooking. It is a blend of fat and flour cooked to a precise point of fragrance and color and is the basis of many hearty local dishes.

24. **Tabasco**® A liquid form of cayenne made from red peppers grown on Avery Island, Louisiana by the McIlhenney Co.

25. **Tasso** A very highly seasoned Cajun smoked ham that has been cured with special seasonings. It is hard, if not impossible to find outside of the New Orleans region.

26. **Uptown and Downtown—West Bank and East Bank** Because the Mississippi River bends and winds and doubles back to form a horseshoe east of the city, it is difficult to use standard directions, north, east, south and west, in New Orleans. Locals use the designations uptown, downtown, river, and lake to make the distinctions. Therefore, uptown includes the area upriver from Canal Street, which is the area to the south of the river side. Downtown is anything to the lake (north) side of Canal Street, but it also refers to the business district. If this is at all confusing, then finding out that West Bank is really to the east of the city will only complicate matters—so forget about it.

27. **Vieux Carré (View-Karaý)** Literally means, "old square" or "old section." It is another name for the French Quarter which was the original city.

There are a few terms and expressions that may not appear in this book, but are defined here to help understand the "Legends of Louisiana Cookbook" and New Orleans itself.

1. **The Big Easy/The City That Care Forgot** New Orleans' nicknames for itself. Things here sometimes get done at a snail's pace because people believe in taking life as it comes—"not to worry." This personifies the Cajuns' wonderful attitude about life.

2. **"Go" Cup** One never has to go far without some form of liquid refreshment in this city. Patrons of bars are offered a disposable cup to take their drinks with them if they want that "one for the road."

3. **Streetcar** Green electric coaches (mistakenly called trolley cars by tourists) that run along a track on the median strip.

4. **Neutral Ground** The median strip that separates the road and the streetcar tracks is known as the "neutral ground" to locals. (In fact any median strip is referred to as neutral ground.)

5. **Dressed** No local ever orders a po boy or any sandwich with lettuce, tomato and mayonnaise. One simply orders it "dressed."

6. **Throws** The most unique characteristic of Mardi Gras is the New Orleans tradition of throwing trinkets from the floats. Throws can be beads, baubles, dubloons, plastic cups, and coconuts. Thus the expression "Throw me something Mister," can be heard from the crowds in the street as the procession of floats go by.

Index of Recipes

Tomatoes